Green Matters

Planet Earth · Language · Culture

Schwerpunktthema Abitur Englisch –
Green Matters: Planet Earth · Language · Culture

von Prof. Dr. Uwe Küchler, Tübingen,
und Judith Preiß, Entringen/Ammerbuch

Verlagsredaktion
Aryane Beaudoin, Elke Lehmann (Projektleitung),
Hartmut Tschepe (verantwortlicher Redakteur)

Technische Umsetzung
krauß-verlagsservice, Ederheim/Hürnheim

Layoutkonzept
Ungermeyer – grafische Angelegenheiten, Berlin

Umschlaggestaltung
orangerie grafikdesign, Berlin

Ergänzungsmaterial für Lehrkräfte:
– Handreichungen für den Unterricht   ISBN 978-3-06-036210-3
– Handreichungen für den Unterricht als Download   ISBN 978-3-06-036211-0

www.cornelsen.de

Die Webseiten Dritter, deren Internetadressen in diesem Lehrwerk angegeben sind, wurden vor Drucklegung sorgfältig geprüft. Der Verlag übernimmt keine Gewähr für die Aktualität und den Inhalt dieser Seiten oder solcher, die mit ihnen verlinkt sind.

1. Auflage, 1. Druck 2020

Alle Drucke dieser Auflage sind inhaltlich unverändert und können im Unterricht nebeneinander verwendet werden.

Druck: AZ Druck und Datentechnik GmbH, Kempten

ISBN 978-3-06-036209-7

PEFC zertifiziert
Dieses Produkt stammt aus nachhaltig
bewirtschafteten Wäldern und kontrollierten
Quellen.

www.pefc.de

PEFC/04-31-2260

Contents

Chapter IV The Art of Saving the Planet

Info boxes (in alphabetical order)

acrostic 26	environmental	metaphor and	onomatopoeia 78
Anthropocene 77	awareness 36	simile 33	review 41
atmosphere 56	greenwashing 42	mockumentary 73	style 13
ecocriticism 55	hero/heroine 14	nature writing 46	tone 64
enumeration 27	IPCC 74		

Abbreviations and symbols

adj	adjective
cf.	compare
f./ff.	and the following page(s)/line(s)
fml	formal
infml	informal
jdm., jdn.	*jemandem, jemanden*
l., ll.	line, lines
n	noun
p., pp.	page, pages
pl	plural
sb.	somebody
sth.	something
v	verb

📄⊙ **cornelsen.de**
➕◁) **Code: xxxxx**

The webcode xxxxx can be entered at www.cornelsen.de to connect you directly to the website you want.

◁) Listening task (audio available)

⊙ Viewing task (video available)

Chapter I

Taking Action for the Environment

Part A
What are the driving forces?

A1 Going beyond hope *Derrick Jensen*

Rather than being in fear or in despair about what the world has come to, many of us are hoping for a change for the better. But what if hope is not helpful at all?

1 a **Think:** Before reading the text on pp. 6–7, think about your personal hopes regarding climate change and the future. Take notes.
   b **Pair:** Compare your hopes with a partner.
   c **Share:** Speaking Present your hopes to the class.

In the essay on the following two pages, US author and environmentalist Derrick Jensen (born 1960) pushes readers to do a lot more than just hope for a better future. Read the text and work on the tasks on pp. 8–9.

The most common words I hear spoken by any environmentalists anywhere are, *We're fucked*. Most of these environmentalists are fighting desperately, using whatever tools they have – or rather whatever legal tools they have, which means whatever
5 tools those in power grant them the right to use, which means whatever tools will be ultimately ineffective – to try to protect some piece of ground, to try to stop the manufacture or release of poisons, to try to stop civilized humans from tormenting some group of plants or animals. Sometimes they're reduced
10 to trying to protect just one tree. […]

But no matter what environmentalists do, our best efforts are insufficient. We're losing badly, on every front. Those in power are hell-bent on destroying the planet, and most people don't care.

15 Frankly, I don't have much hope. But I think that's a good thing. Hope is what keeps us chained to the system, the conglomerate of people and ideas and ideals that is causing the destruction of the Earth.

To start, there is the false hope that suddenly somehow the system may inexplicably change. Or technology will save us. […] All of these
20 false hopes lead to inaction, or at least to ineffectiveness. […] False hopes bind us to unlivable situations, and blind us to real possibilities. […]

If only we get a Democrat in the White House, things will be okay. If only we pass this or that piece of legislation, things will be okay. If only we defeat this or that piece of legislation, things will be okay.
25 Nonsense. Things will not be okay. They're already not ok and they're getting worse. Rapidly.

But it isn't only false hopes that keep those who go along enchained. It is hope itself. Hope, we are told, is our beacon in the dark. It is our light at the end of a long, dark tunnel. It is the beam of light that
30 makes its way into our prison cells. It is our reason for persevering, our protection against despair (which must be avoided at all costs). […]

Hope is, in fact, a curse, a bane. I say this not only because of the lovely Buddhist saying 'Hope and fear chase each other's tails,' not only because hope leads us away from the present, away from who
35 and where we are right now and toward some imaginary future state. I say this because of *what hope* is. […]

To hope for some result means you have given up any agency concerning it. Many people say they hope the dominant culture stops destroying the world. By saying that, they've assumed that
40 the destruction will continue, at least in the short term, and they've stepped away from their own ability to participate in stopping it. […]

When we realize the degree of agency we actually do have, we no longer have to 'hope' at all. We simply do the work. We make sure salmon survive. We make sure prairie dogs survive. We make sure
45 grizzlies survive. We do whatever it takes.

[8] **torment sb.** [tɔːˈment] (fml) make sb. suffer
[12] **insufficient** [ˌɪnsəˈfɪʃnt] not enough
[13] **hell-bent on doing sth.** *wild entschlossen, etwas zu tun*
[16] **conglomerate** [kənˈɡlɒmərət] *Zusammenschluss*
[23] **legislation** [ˌledʒɪsˈleɪʃn] law
[24] **defeat sb./sth.** cause sb./sth. to fail
[28] **beacon** light or fire used as a signal or warning
[30] **persevere** [ˌpɜːsəˈvɪə] continue trying to do sth. difficult
[31] **despair** [dɪˈspeə] condition of hopelessness
[32] **curse** magic spell to bring bad luck
bane something causing trouble or worry
[37] **agency** [ˈeɪdʒənsi] capacity to act
[44] **salmon** [ˈsæmən] *Lachs*

When we stop hoping for external assistance, when we stop hoping that the awful situation we're in will somehow resolve itself, when we stop hoping the situation will somehow not get worse, then we are finally free – truly free – to honestly start working to resolve it. I
50 would say that when hope dies, action begins. [...]

A wonderful thing happens when you give up on hope, which is that you realize you never needed it in the first place. You realize that giving up on hope didn't kill you. It didn't even make you less effective. In fact it made you more effective, because you ceased
55 relying on someone or something else to solve your problems – you ceased *hoping* your problems would somehow get solved through the magical assistance of God, the Great Mother, the Sierra Club, valiant tree-sitters, brave salmon, or even the Earth itself – and you just began doing whatever it takes to solve those problems yourself.
60 When you give up on hope, something even better happens that is not killing you, which is that in some sense it does kill you. You die. [...] The socially constructed you died. The civilized you died. The manufactured, fabricated, stamped, molded you died. The victim died.

And who is left when that you dies? You are left. Animal you.
65 Naked you. Vulnerable (and invulnerable) you. Mortal you. Survivor you. The you who thinks not what the culture taught you to think but what you think. The you who feels not what the culture taught you to feel but what you feel. The you who is not who the culture taught you to be but who you are. The you who can say *yes*, the you who can say
70 *no*. The you who is a part of the land where you live. The you who will fight (or not) to defend your family. The you who will fight (or not) to defend those you love. The you who will fight (or not) to defend the land upon which your life and the lives of those you love depends. [...]

When you give up on hope, you turn away from fear.
75 And when you quit relying on hope, and instead begin to protect the people, things, and places you love, you become very dangerous indeed to those in power.

In case you're wondering, that's a very good thing.

From: Derrick Jensen, 'Beyond Hope', in: Orion Magazine, May–June 2006

---

54 cease doing sth. [siːs] stop doing sth.
57 valiant ['væliənt] very brave
63 mold (AE)/**mould** (BE) **sb./sth.** give sb./sth. a particular form, strongly influence sb./sth.
65 vulnerable ['vʌlnərəbl] easily hurt or attacked

Comprehension

2 a Summarize Derrick Jensen's view of the connection of hope and environmental activism in no more than three sentences.

 b Read your summary to a partner and listen to his/hers.

 c Compare your summaries.

Analysis

3 List and contrast the positive and negative effects of hope that are described in the text. Don't forget to give line numbers.

Hope			
Positive effects	**Line(s)**	**Negative effects**	**Line(s)**
– connects us to other people and society	ll. 16–17	– keeps us chained to the system	l. 16

Beyond the text

4 a Conduct a survey among friends and family members to find out which concept of hope they have.

 b Speaking Give a short presentation of your results to the class.

5 **Writing** You have been asked to contribute to an online forum by comparing Derrick Jensen's understanding of hope to your own. In no more than 250 words, comment on whether you agree or disagree with his views. Emphasize your argumentation with examples.

Language help

It seems to me (that) … · In my opinion … · As far as I am concerned, … · I understand (that) … · My personal view is (that) … · From my point of view … · It is claimed (that) … · I must admit (that) … · I am (not) sure/convinced/certain (that) … · I think/believe/suppose (that) … · Not only this, but I also think (that) … · On the one hand, … · On the other hand, … · Let me give you an example. · Firstly, I would like to say/mention (that) … · The writer argues (that) …

A2 The role of the environmental movement
Naomi Klein

Environmental awareness seems to be a fairly recent phenomenon. But is that true? When did people begin to think about the environment? When did they rally and start changing their behaviour to protect, save and improve it?

You are going to read an excerpt from the book *This Changes Everything* (2014) by Canadian scholar and activist Naomi Klein (born 1970). She outlines the development of the environmental movement and its close ties to Western capitalist societies.
Read her text and work on the tasks on pp. 12–13.

There is one other group that might have provided a challenge to Western culture's disastrous view of nature as a bottomless vending machine. That group, of course, is the environmental movement, the network of organizations that exists to protect the natural world from

5 being devoured by human activity. And yet the movement has not played this role, at least not in a sustained and coherent manner.

In part, that has to do with the movement's unusually elite history, particularly in North America. When conservationism emerged as a powerful force in the late nineteenth and early twentieth centuries,

10 it was primarily about men of privilege who enjoyed fishing, hunting, camping, and hiking and who recognized that many of their favorite wilderness spots were under threat from the rapid expansion of industrialization. For the most part, these men did not call into question the frenetic economic project that was devouring natural landscapes

15 all over the continent – they simply wanted to make sure that some

---

[2] **vending machine** machine that sells snacks, drinks or cigarettes

[5] **devour sth.** [dɪˈvaʊə] (here) destroy sth.

[14] **frenetic** [frəˈnetɪk] moving or acting in a very excited or energetic manner

particularly spectacular pockets were set aside for their recreation and aesthetic appreciation. [...]

There were those in the movement, however, who saw in the threats to their country's most beautiful places signs of
20 a deeper cultural crisis. For instance, John Muir, the great naturalist writer who helped found the Sierra Club in 1892, excoriated the industrialists who dammed wild rivers and drowned beautiful valleys. To him they were heathens – 'devotees of ravaging commercialism' who 'instead of lifting
25 their eyes to the God of the mountains, lift them to the Almighty Dollar.'

He was not the only heretic. A strain of radicalism drove some of the early Western ecological thinkers to argue for doing more than protecting isolated landscapes. [...]
30 These ideas were hugely influential in the evolution of ecological thought, but unattached to populist movements, they posed little threat to galloping industrialization. The dominant worldview continued to see humans as a conquering army, subduing and mechanizing the natural world. Even so, by the 1930s, with socialism on the rise around
35 the world, the more conservative elements of the growing environmental movement sought to distance themselves from [the] 'radical' suggestion that nature had an inherent value beyond its utility to man. [...]

By the time Rachel Carson published *Silent Spring* in 1962, the
40 attempts to turn nature into a mere cog in the American industrial machine had grown so aggressive, so overtly militaristic, that it was no longer possible to pretend that combining capitalism with conservation was simply a matter of protecting a few pockets of green. Carson's book boiled over with righteous condemnations of a chemical industry
45 that used aerial bombardment to wipe out insects, thoughtlessly endangering human and animal life in the process. [...]

'The "control of nature,"' Carson wrote, 'is a phrase conceived in arrogance, born of the Neanderthal age of biology and philosophy, when it was supposed that nature exists for
50 the convenience of man. ... It is our alarming misfortune that so primitive a science has armed itself with the most modern and terrible weapons, and that in turning them against the insects it has also turned them against the earth.'

Carson's writing inspired a new, much more radical gener-
55 ation of environmentalists to see themselves as part of a fragile planetary ecosystem rather than as its engineers or mechanics, giving birth to the field of Ecological Economics. It was in this context that the underlying logic of extractivisim – that there would always be more earth for us to consume
60 – began to be forcefully challenged within the mainstream.

John Muir (1838–1914), Scottish-American naturalist who is credited with being the 'Father of the National Parks' (cf. Chapter III, pp. 65–66)

22 **excoriate sb.** [ɪkˈskɔːrieɪt] (fml) strongly criticize sb.
23 **heathen** [ˈhiːðn] Heide/-in, Ungläubige(r)
24 **devotee of sth.** [ˌdevəˈtiː] person who is very interested in and admires sth.
   ravage [ˈrævɪdʒ] cause damage (to sth.)
27 **heretic** [ˈherətɪk] Ketzer/in, Andersgläubige(r)
33 **subdue sth.** [səbˈdjuː] reduce the force of sth.
36 **seek to do, sought, sought** (fml) try to do
40 **a mere cog** lediglich ein (Zahn-)Rädchen
44 **condemnation of sth.** [ˌkɒndemˈneɪʃn] expression of strong criticism of sth.
48 **conceive sth.** [kənˈsiːv] (here) imagine sth.

Rachel Carlson (1907–1964), US biologist and writer, with her book Silent Spring (cf. Chapter III, pp. 59–60)

The pinnacle of the debate came in 1972 when the Club of Rome published *The Limits to Growth*, a runaway best-seller that used early computer models to predict that if natural systems continued to be depleted at their current rate, humanity would overshoot the planet's
65 carrying capacity by the middle of the twenty-first century. Saving a few beautiful mountain ranges wouldn't be enough to get us out of this fix; the logic of growth itself needed to be confronted. […]

And yet in the most powerful parts of the environmental movement, in the key decades during which we have been confronting the climate
70 threat, these voices of warning have gone unheeded. The movement did not reckon with limits of growth in an economic system built on maximizing profits, it instead tried to prove that saving the planet could be a great new business opportunity.

The reasons for this political timidity have plenty to do with the
75 themes already discussed: the power and allure of free market logic that usurped so much intellectual life in the late 1980s and 1990s, including large parts of the conservation movement. But this persistent unwillingness to follow science to its conclusions also speaks to the power of the cultural narrative that tells us that humans are ultimately
80 in control of the earth, not the other way around. This is the same narrative that assures us that, however bad things get, we are going to be saved at the last minute – whether by the market, by philanthropic billionaires, or by technological wizards – or best of all, by all three at the same time. And while we wait, we keep digging in deeper.

85 Only when we dispense with these various forms of magical thinking will we be ready to leave extractivism behind and build the societies we need within the boundaries we have […].

From: Naomi Klein, This Changes Everything. Capitalism vs the Climate, *2014*

61 **pinnacle of sth.** ['pɪnəkl] most important or exciting part of sth.
64 **deplete sth.** [dɪ'pliːt] (fml) reduce sth. drastically
70 **go unheeded** (fml) be heard but then ignored
71 **reckon with sth.** regard sth. as a serious problem
74 **timidity** [tɪ'mɪdəti] being shy and nervous
75 **allure** [ə'lʊə] attractiveness
76 **usurp sth.** [juː'zɜːp] (fml) take control of sth. without permission
77 **persistent** [pə'sɪstən] long-lasting
82 **philanthropic** [ˌfɪlən'θrɒpɪk] (adj) supporting society or public life financially

Protest banner at the Youth Strike for Climate demonstration in London, February 2020

Comprehension

1 Choose whether the following statements are true or false and give evidence (line numbers) from the text. If they are false, correct them.

Statement	True	False	Line(s)
A Western culture sees nature as a very fragile system that needs to be protected. Correction: _____	○	○	
B Fishermen and hunters started the environmental movement in the late 19th century. Correction: _____	○	○	
C John Muir criticized the growing commercialization of society. Correction: _____	○	○	
D The logic of growth is the main argument for the protection of forests. Correction: _____	○	○	
E People profoundly believe in controlling nature and the climate crisis. Correction: _____	○	○	

2 Work with a partner. Explain the terms 'conservationism' (l. 8) and 'extractivism' (l. 86) based on the excerpt from Naomi Klein's book on pp. 9–11. Use your own words.

Analysis

3 Describe why the warnings of the environmental movement were ignored at different stages of its development.

4 Analyse Naomi Klein's use of language and style to create an impact on the reader (→ Info box, p. 13).

Info Style

Style is the way in which a text is written. In general, style refers to the language that the writer uses to convey a message. In order to examine the style of a text, it is necessary to examine aspects such as

- **diction:** the choice of words, e. g. certain fields of words, descriptive adjectives or verbs of motion
- **tone:** the way that a writer treats his or her topic (the tone can be intimate, detached, distanced, angry, solemn, informal, jocular, serious, ironic, humorous, neutral)
- **register:** the level of language (formal, neutral, informal)
- **syntax:** e.g. sentence structure, active or passive voice
- **stylistic elements:** methods and techniques (e. g. metaphors, personification, alliteration) used to produce a particular effect

Furthermore, the style of a text can be shaped by the way the information is organized and presented (**layout**).

Beyond the text

5 **Writing** Comment on the current status of the environmental movement and the consequences this could have for the future. Compare your own opinion with statements from the text.

6 The editorial board of a magazine wants to find out about people's views on climate change and the future of our society. It has organized a panel discussion on the topic 'Apocalypse now? How do we start into the new decade?'. The following six guests are participating:

- a journalist, who is the host of the panel discussion
- a student
- a green politician
- a business leader
- a philanthropist [fɪˈlænθrəpɪst]
- a scientist

Split up in groups of six. Each group member chooses one of the roles.

a Follow the instructions on the role card your teacher will give you and prepare the role play.

b **Speaking** Act out the role play with the other members of your group.

Part B
Putting up resistance

B1 The making of a heroine

1 What is your idea of a hero/heroine? Give a short definition.

Robin Hood, legendary English folk hero and champion of the poor

Info Hero [ˈhɪərəʊ]**/Heroine** [ˈherəʊɪn]
Interestingly, the idea of a hero or heroine is historically derived from a **shepherd**, somebody who protects a herd (of sheep), guides it to green pastures and defends it against internal or external danger. It is not difficult to see
5 the analogy between a shepherd and an individual with special, unusual gifts who fights for order and justice, and defends the community against chaos, villains or any other perceived threat.
Nations tend to create **national or war heroes/heroines**,
10 but they do not have to be warriors in the literal sense. In religious contexts, heroes/heroines are often praised as **saints** and become **role models** for the community.
Heroes/Heroines can be found in all cultures and they usually have a special place in the memory and cultural narratives, even though that may occur a long time after their death.
15 Conventionally, typical features of a hero/heroine are those of **winners** – of people coming out on top. They are perceived as brave and determined to pursue and attain a goal (the protection of their community). Heroes/Heroines – whether in the cultural life of a community, a film, a novel or a song – decide to act in the face of difficulty rather than remain a pawn of their circumstances. For their agency and perseverance, they get the admiration and praise from
20 their peers, community or society, and become the centre of attention.
However, the notion of who is praised as a hero/heroine (and who is not) changes over time. Some heroes/heroines remain **'unsung'** during their lifetime and get admiration and accolades by later generations. Each generation reaffirms its heroes/heroines or creates new ones.

From schoolgirl to warrior *Jonathan Watts*

In 2019, a 17-year-old schoolgirl who used to be bullied because of a developmental disorder suddenly became an international heroine to many people and rallied a large social movement behind her. How did it happen? What does it take to influence the course of the world? Can young or weak people have just as much of an impact on others?

Read the following newspaper article from March 2019 about the young Swedish climate activist Greta Thunberg and her unexpected rise to international fame. Then work on the tasks on pp. 17–19.

2 Before reading, describe your impression of Greta Thunberg based on the two photos on the right.

Greta Thunberg (born 2003 in Stockholm, Sweden) during her solo school strike for the climate outside the Parliament building in Stockholm in September 2018

Greta Thunberg cut a frail and lonely figure when she started a school strike for the climate outside the Swedish parliament building last August [2018].
5 Her parents tried to dissuade her. Classmates declined to join. Passers-by expressed pity and bemusement at the sight of the then unknown 15-year-old sitting on the cobblestones with a
10 hand-painted banner.

Eight months on, the picture could not be more different. The pigtailed teenager is feted across the world as a model of determination, inspiration and
15 positive action. National presidents and corporate executives line up to be criti-cised by her, face to face. Her *skolstrejk för klimatet* (school strike for climate) banner has been translated into dozens
20 of languages. And, most striking of all, the loner is now anything but alone.

On 15 March [2019], when she returns to the cobblestones (as she has done almost every Friday in rain, sun,
25 ice and snow), it will be as a figurehead

Greta Thunberg with more than 10,000 school students in a school climate strike in Lausanne, Switzerland, in January 2020

for a vast and growing movement. The global climate strike this Friday is gearing up to be one of the biggest environmental protests the world has ever seen. As it approaches, Thunberg is clearly excited.

'It's amazing,' she says. 'It's more than 71 countries and more than
30 700 places, and counting. It's increasing very much now, and that's very, very fun.'

A year ago [in 2018], this was unimaginable. Back then, Thunberg was a painfully introverted, slightly built nobody, waking at 6am to prepare for school and heading back home at 3pm. 'Nothing really was
35 happening in my life,' she recalls. 'I have always been that girl in the back who doesn't say anything. I thought I couldn't make a difference because I was too small.'

She was never quite like the other kids. Her mother, Malena Ernman, is one of Sweden's most celebrated opera singers. Her father, Svante
40 Thunberg, is an actor and author (named after Svante Arrhenius, the Nobel prize-winning scientist who in 1896 first calculated how carbon

[1] **frail** weak or thin
[5] **dissuade sb.** [dɪˈsweɪd] convince sb. not to do sth.
[6] **decline to do sth.** (fml) say no when sb. wants you to do sth.
[12] **pigtailed** wearing her hair in pigtails (*Zöpfe*)
[13] **be feted** [ˈfeɪtɪd] (fml) be celebrated or honoured
[14] **determination** [dɪˌtɜːmɪˈneɪʃn] strong desire and effort to do sth., especially against difficulty
[16] **corporate** [ˈkɔːpərət] (adj) belonging to a large business
[25] **figurehead** [ˈfɪɡəhed] symbolic leader without actual power or authority

dioxide emissions could lead to the greenhouse effect). Greta was exceptionally bright. Four years ago, she was diagnosed with Asperger's.

'I overthink. Some people can just let things go, but I can't, especially
45 if there's something that worries me or makes me sad. I remember when I was younger, and in school, our teachers showed us films of plastic in the ocean, starving polar bears and so on. I cried through all the movies. My classmates were concerned when they watched the film, but when it stopped, they started thinking about other things. I
50 couldn't do that. Those pictures were stuck in my head.' […]

Her parents were the guinea pigs. She discovered she had remarkable powers of persuasion, and her mother gave up flying, which had a severe impact on her career. Her father became a vegetarian. As well as feeling relieved by the transformation of their formerly quiet and
55 morose daughter, they say they were persuaded by her reasoning. 'Over the years, I ran out of arguments,' says her father. 'She kept

---

'I thought I couldn't make a difference because I was too small.'

---

showing us documentaries, and we read books together. Before that, I really didn't have a clue. I thought we had the climate issue sorted,' he says. 'She changed us and now she is changing a great many other
60 people. There was no hint of this in her childhood. It's unbelievable. If this can happen, anything can happen.'

The climate strike was inspired by students from the Parkland school in Florida, who walked out of classes in protest against the US gun laws that enabled the massacre on their campus. Greta was part of a group
65 that wanted to do something similar to raise awareness about climate change, but they couldn't agree what. Last summer, after a record heatwave in northern Europe and forest fires that ravaged swathes of Swedish land up to the Arctic, Thunberg decided to go it alone. Day one was 20 August 2018.

70 'I painted the sign on a piece of wood and, for the flyers, wrote down some facts I thought everyone should know. And then I took my bike to the parliament and just sat there,' she recalls. 'The first day, I sat alone from about 8.30am to 3pm – the regular schoolday. And then on the
75 second day, people started joining me. After that, there were people there all the time.'

From: Jonathan Watts: 'Greta Thunberg, schoolgirl climate change warrior: "Some people can let things go. I can't."', theguardian.com, 11 March 2019

---

43 Asperger's (syndrome) [ˈæspɜːɡəz ˌsɪndrəʊm] mild form of autism [ˈɔːtɪzəm] causing difficulty with social interaction and communication

51 guinea pig [ˈɡɪni pɪɡ] (here) person used in an experiment („Versuchskaninchen")

52 powers of persuasion [pəˈsweɪʒn] ability to make sb. do sth., especially by giving them reasons why they should

55 morose [məˈrəʊs] unhappy, silent and bad-tempered

67 ravage sth. [ˈrævɪdʒ] destroy or damage sth. badly

68 swathe [sweɪð] (fml) long thin strip of sth., usually land or lawn

Comprehension

3 The table below lists descriptions of Greta Thunberg's personality from the newspaper article on pp. 15–16. Explain the meaning of each phrase in your own words and decide whether you consider the given trait to be a strength or a weakness (tick one of the two boxes).

Description of Greta	Meaning	Strength	Weakness
a frail figure (ll. 1–2)	*a body that does not seem very strong, not muscular*	○	✓
a lonely figure (ll. 1–2)		○	○
a model of determination (l. 14)		○	○
a model of inspiration (l. 14)		○	○
a loner, no longer alone (l. 21)		○	○
a figurehead for a growing movement (ll. 25–26)		○	○

Description of Greta	Meaning	Strength	Weakness
a painfully introverted nobody (l. 33)		○	○
the girl in the back (ll. 35–36)		○	○
never quite like other kids (l. 38)		○	○
exceptionally bright (ll. 42–43)		○	○
diagnosed with Asperger's (l. 43)		○	○
overthinking, worrying (ll. 44–45)		○	○
has powers of persuasion (l. 52)		○	○
transformation from formerly morose daughter (ll. 54–55)		○	○

Analysis

4 a Discuss the following statement:

What seems like a strength to one person may be a weakness to another.

b With a partner, look back at which personality traits you listed as strengths and which ones you listed as weaknesses in **3**. Think of some negative aspects for each strength, and think of some positive aspects for each weakness.

5 Examine the language and style (→ Info box, p. 13) Jonathan Watts uses in order to give a balanced portrait of Greta Thunberg. List some features and formulations that are typical of newspaper articles.

Beyond the text

6 **Viewing** Your teacher will play the video of a speech by Greta Thunberg. While watching, examine how Thunberg uses body language (gestures and facial expressions) and tone of voice to send her message.

7 a Interview or research a person who made a difference in your community. This person could be a former student of your school, an activist, a politician, a teacher, an artist, a musician, a media personality, maybe even a member of your family. Gather enough information to answer the following questions:
  – How does the person live? Think of their daily activities.
  – Which characteristics set this person apart? What are their talents?
  – What experiences have they had? What single most important moment drove them to act or do something differently? Did they have to overcome adversity and/or experience failures?
  – How did that person make a difference? How could that make them a 'hero/heroine'?

b **Writing** Write a short portrait of the person you have chosen based on the information you gathered in **a**.

c **Speaking** Group up in teams of four and give a short presentation of your hero/heroine to the others. Take notes on the other heroes/heroines presented.

d Compare the characteristics of all the heroes/heroines that were presented.

8 **Mediating** During the COVID-19 pandemic in 2020, some media published features on *Helden des Alltags*. Your friend Jenny, who is originally from Canada, asks what is meant by *Helden des Alltags* and how the expression could be translated into English. Write a short email or chat message in which you explain *Helden des Alltags* to her. Don't forget to use examples.

9 Work on either **a** or **b**.

a Discuss what it takes to 'save the planet'. List personality traits that you think are needed to solve (some of) our environmental crises.

b Comment on the personality traits of 'environmental villains'. What should an 'environmental hero/heroine' be like to fight them?

Make sure you understand these words and phrases from Greta's speech:
– mass extinction
– eternal economic growth
– urgency
– irreversible chain reaction
– tipping point
– equity
– IPCC = Intergovernmental Panel on Climate Change (cf. Chapter IV, p. 74)
– mature
– betrayal

B2 Advice to myself #2: Resistance *Louise Erdrich*

One of the most renowned US writers, Louise Erdrich (born 1954), reflects on advice that she would give herself when it comes to being in this world and resisting what seems required.
Read her poem and work on the tasks on pp. 22–23.

Resist the thought that you may need a savior,
or another special being to walk beside you.
Resist the thought that you are alone.
Resist turning your back on the knife
5   of the world's sorrow,
resist turning that knife upon yourself.
Resist your disappearance
into sentimental monikers,
into the violent pattern of corporate logos,
10   into the mouth of the unholy flower of consumerism.
Resist being consumed.
Resist your disappearance
into anything except
the face you had before you walked up to the podium.
15   Resist all funding sources but accept all money.
Cut the strings and dismantle the web
that needing money throws over you.
Resist the distractions of excess.
Wear old clothes and avoid chain restaurants.
20   Resist your genius and your own significance
as declared by others.
Resist all hint of glory but accept the accolades
as tributes to your double.
Walk away in your unpurchased skin.
25   Resist the millionth purchase and go backward.
Get rid of everything.
If you exist, then you are loved
by existence. What do you need?
A spoon, a blanket, a bowl, a book –
30   maybe the book you give away.
Resist the need to worry, robbing everything
of immediacy and peace.
Resist traveling except where you want to go.
Resist seeing yourself in others or them in you.
35   Nothing, everything, is personal.
Resist all pressure to have children
unless you crave the torment of joy.

¹ **savior** (AE)/**saviour** (BE) [ˈseɪvjə] person who rescues sb. from harmful or dangerous situations
⁵ **sorrow** sadness or grief
⁸ **moniker** [ˈmɒnɪkə] (infml) joking name you give to sb. or to yourself, nickname
¹⁰ **unholy** awful, terrible, profane
¹¹ **consume sth./sb.** [kənˈsjuːm] use sth./sb., (here) exploit sth./sb.
²² **accolade** [ˈækəleɪd] (fml) admiration and appreciation for sb.
²³ **tribute to sth.** [ˈtrɪbjuːt] showing respect and high esteem for sth.

If you give in to irrationality, then
resist cleaning up the messes your children make.

40 You are robbing them of small despairs they can fix.
Resist cleaning up after your husband.
It will soon replace having sex with him.
Resist outrageous charts spelling doom.
However you can, rely on sun and wind.

45 Resist loss of the miraculous
by lowering your standards
for what constitutes a miracle.
It is all a fucking miracle.
Resist your own gift's power

50 to tear you away from the simplicity of tears.
Your gift will begin to watch you having your emotions,
so that it can use them in an interesting paragraph,
or to get a laugh.
Resist the blue chair of dreams, the red chair of science, the black chair of the humanities,

55 and just be human.
Resist all chairs.
Be the one sitting on the ground
or perching on the beam overhead
or sleeping beneath the podium.

60 Resist disappearing from the stage,
unless you can walk straight into the bathroom and resume the face,
the desolate face, the radiant face, the weary face, the face
that has become your own, though all your life
you have resisted it.

43 spell doom *den Untergang ankündigen*
58 perch on sth. (infml) sit on sth. with a good overview
62 desolate ['dɛsələt] (adj) feeling very sad and lonely
radiant ['reɪdiənt] (adj) full of happiness or beauty
weary ['wɪəri] (adj) tired, exhausted, possibly bored

From: 'Women and Standing Rock' in: Orion Magazine, 35th Anniversary Issue 2017

All the words[1] from the poem

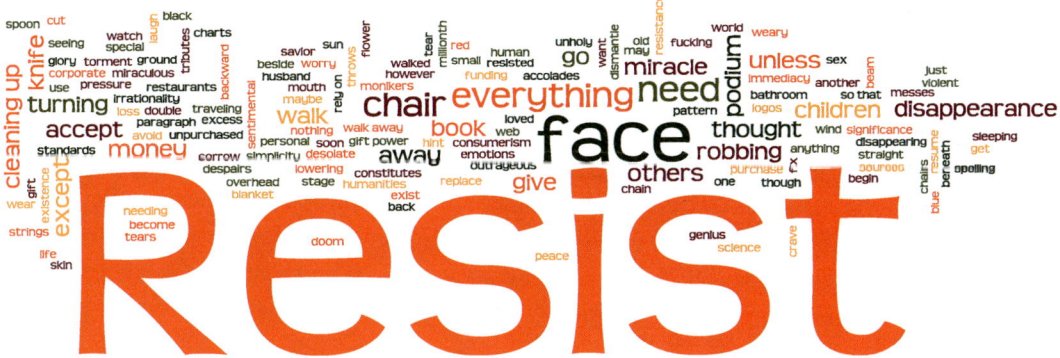

___

[1] The size of a word in the word cloud is proportional to the number of times the word appears in the poem.

Comprehension

1 State who is addressed in this poem.

2 Summarize what is to be resisted.

Analysis

3 Complete the table below. Use the poet's words, images and phrases
  listed in the left column to consider how their meaning relates to the
  environment / the natural world.

Words/Images/ Phrases	General meaning	Environmental interpretation
'savior, or another special being' (ll. 1–2)	no higher power or authority will set us free from our problems	People must not wait for the government or their neighbours to protect, clean, repair the environment or solve problems.
'unholy flower of consumerism' (l. 10)		
'distractions of excess' (l. 18)		

'get rid of everything' (l. 26)		
'traveling except where you want to go' (l. 33)		
'Nothing, everything is personal' (l. 35)		
'charts spelling doom' (l. 43)		
'loss of the miraculous' (l. 45)		

Beyond the text

4 a In small groups, go back to the points of resistance you gathered in **2**. Brainstorm similarities and differences to your own life, to society's expectations and to reasons why we could or should resist these issues.

   b Speaking Give a short presentation of your results to the class.

Chapter II

Being Aware of the Natural Environment

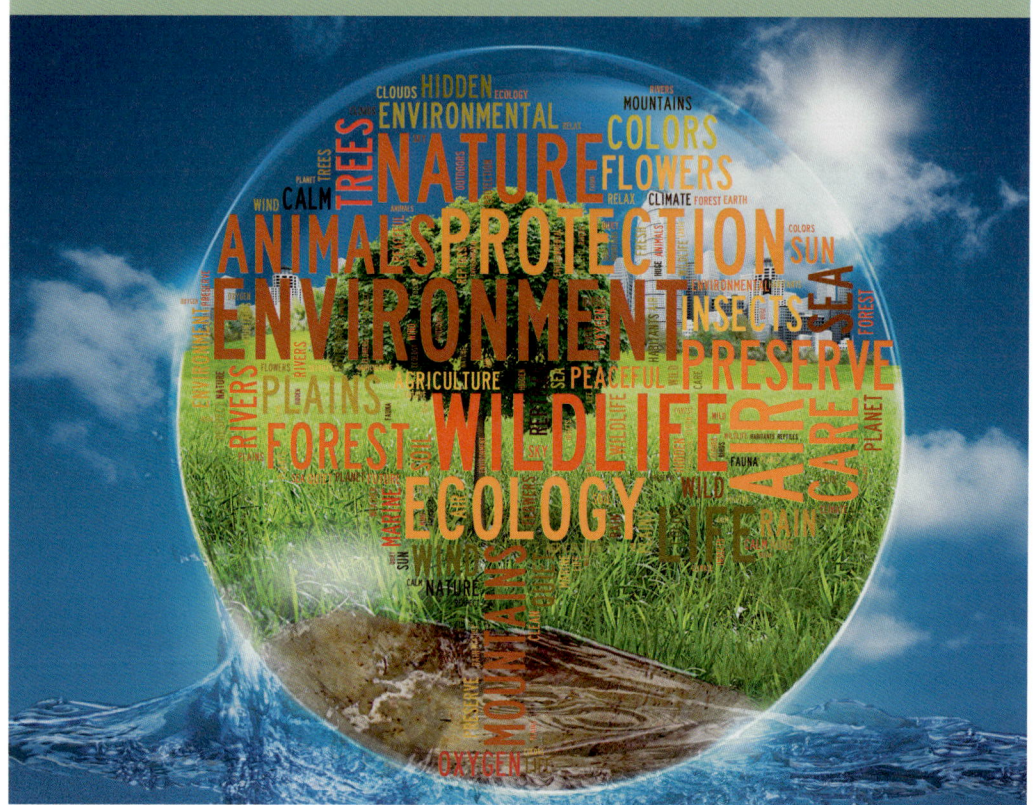

Part A
Taking a leaf out of nature's book

A1 Describing the natural world
Robert Macfarlane

Environmental destruction, pollution and the loss of landscapes may impoverish our language too: If we lose the name or word for something, we also lose its meaning.

By spelling out the names of plants and animals in a poetic way, British nature writer Robert Macfarlane (born 1976) casts a spell on us, on our language and on our environmental awareness (→ Info box, p. 36). Read the four poems on the opposite page and work on the tasks on p. 26.

acorn

As flake is to blizzard, as
Curve is to sphere,[2] as knot is to net, as
One is to many, as coin is to money, as
    bird is to flock,[4] as
5 Rock is to mountain, as drop is to fountain, as
    spring is to river, as glint[6] is to glitter, as
Near is to far, as wind is to weather, as
    feather is to flight, as light is to star, as
    kindness is to good, so acorn is to wood.

[2] **sphere** [sfɪə]
    Kreisfläche, Kugel
[4] **flock** group of birds (or sheep), figuratively also used for humans
[6] **glint** bright, brilliant reflection of light on a surface

fern

Fern's first form is furled,[1]
Each frond[2] fast as a fiddle-head.
Reach, roll and unfold follows.
    Fern *flares.*[4]
5 Now fern is fully fanned.[5]

[1] **furl sth.** roll sth. into a tight spiral
[2] **frond** *Farnkrautwedel*
    fiddle-head *Geigenschnecke, Geigenkopf*
[4] **flare** (here) become wider
[5] **fan (out)** spread out

ivy

I am ivy, a real high-flyer.
Via bark and stone I scale[2] tree and spire.
You call me ground-cover; I say sky-wire.[3]

[2] **scale sth.** (fml) (here) climb to the top of sth.
    spire top of a tower
[3] **wire** *Draht, Kabel*

magpie

Magpie Manifesto:
Argue Every Toss![2]
Gossip,[3] Bicker, Yak and Snicker All Day Long!
Pick a Fight[4] in an Empty Room!
5 Interrupt, Interject, Intercept, Intervene!
Every Magpie for Every Magpie against
    Every Other Walking Flying Swimming
    Creeping Creature on the Earth!*
    * Except eagles, for they are too scary …

[2] **toss** act of throwing sth.
[3] **gossip** (v) talk about others, often not in a nice way
    bicker argue about sth. unimportant
    yak [jæk] (infml) *quasseln, quatschen*
    snicker silently laugh, giggle, chuckle
[4] **pick a fight** start a fight or an argument

From: Robert Macfarlane and Jackie Morris, The Lost Words, *2017*

Comprehension

1 Summarize each of the four poems in one or two sentences. What is the plant or animal like?

Analysis

2 Explain what you notice about the form of all four poems. Use the Info box for help.

> **Info Acrostic** (German 'Akrostichon')
> An acrostic is a piece of writing, usually a poem, in which the first letters (sometimes syllables or words) of each line can be read downwards to form a word, name or phrase. Acrostics are often used playfully. But they are also used to aid one's memory or to provide a (somewhat) hidden message, such as on protest posters or in love songs.

3 **a** Describe the effect of using likeness *(A is to B, as C is to D)* in the poem 'acorn'. How does that help to describe the acorn?

   b State what the lines of the poem 'fern' have in common. Name the literary device and describe its function.

   c Describe the effect of using personification *(I am …)* in the poem 'ivy'.

   d Point out what is implied by the term *manifesto* in line 1 of the poem 'magpie'. Consider which punctuation mark comes at the end of each sentence.

4 Examine the form of the individual poems. Look at the rhythm, the length of the lines and the line breaks.

5 **a** Work with a partner. Each partner chooses one of the poems on p. 25 and practises reading it out loud several times – with varying moods in mind (e.g. happy, sad, stressed, confident, insecure, adventurous).

   b Discuss with your partner how your chosen poem changes with every mood you use.

   c **Speaking** Choose the mood that best fits your interpretation of the poem. Perform the reading of your poem for the class. Make sure to perform it in the mood you have chosen.

Beyond the text

6 **a** Think of a plant, an animal or a natural landscape that is endangered. Write down the English word for it. You may look it up in a dictionary.

   b Brainstorm your chosen word and find features that are unique to it.

   c **Writing** Create an acrostic for your word. Write the word down with each line starting with one letter. Then complete your acrostic line by line. Let the style or (rhyme) pattern of the poems on p. 25 inspire you.

A2 7 seeds to start your day *Thor Hanson*

1 Look at the two pictures and describe them. What do they have in common? What comes to your mind when you think about them? Take a few notes. Compare your results with a partner.

The US *Orion Magazine*, which is focused on nature, culture and environmental issues, has a regular feature called 'enumeration' (→ Info box below). Under this rubric it presents interesting or surprising things or facts that 'tell a story'.
Read the enumeration below and work on the tasks on pp. 29–30.

> **Info Enumeration**
> Enumeration is the one-by-one listing of details, words or items. It divides an idea in order to keep things clear for the reader but at the same time creates a feeling of wholeness. It is used to spell out the idea in more detail and express the message in a stronger way.

1. **Douglas Fir.** It begins with firewood, a chunk of straight-grain fir, split small to fit the cookstove. This log started life as a seed, just like the countless trunks and stems that sprawl in all directions outside my window. Seed plants surround us all day long, and so do seeds
5   themselves, fueling us with their stored energy and enriching our lives with their unique abilities to defend, endure, and travel.

2. **Wheat.** Heat from the fir log browns the pancakes made from wheat flour, one form of
10   plant energy cooking another. Whether a grain, nut, pulse, pip, or kernel, botanists call a seed 'a baby plant in a box with its lunch.' Every calorie it contains evolved to fuel the growth of the
15   sprout. So when we eat seeds, are we not stealing the food intended for babies?

[1] **fir** *Tanne*
straight-grain (adj) *geradefaserig*
[3] **trunk** *Baumstamm*
stem *Baumstamm*
sprawl grow wildly
[5] **fuel sb./sth.** provide food for sb., make sth. increase
[7] **wheat** *Weizen*
[9] **flour** ['flaʊə] *Mehl*
[11] **pulses** (usually pl) *Hülsenfrüchte*
[12] **pip** seed found inside some fruit
[15] **sprout** small plant at its beginning, baby plant

3. Cotton. My son comes to the table in striped pajamas, trailing a stuffed snake sewn from an old shirt. In other words, he is adorned
20 with more than eight miles of yarn spun from the seed coats of a plant the Romans called *gossypium*, the Arabs named *qutun*, and we

know as cotton. We now wrap this seed fluff that evolved to waft on wind and wave around our bodies in every imaginable shape and
25 shade – my jeans and flannel are more of the same. Sometimes we let cotton move us too, woven into sails and spinnakers, and strung from the masts of ships.

4. Coffee. Drip by drip it slowly fills mugs, the yellow one for me and the tall blue one for
30 my wife. Legend credits this beverage to an Ethiopian goatherd whose flock ate the seeds

and began to dance. Scientists think the caffeine in coffee evolved as a pesticide, an herbicide, or perhaps even a memory-enhancer for bees. For once I don't care why – I'm just thankful it's ready.

35 **5. Pepper.** Bacon sizzles in a skillet, crusted with the seeds of an Indian rainforest vine. Peppercorns once anchored a global spice trade that funded empires and drove the explorations of Magellan and Columbus. But this morning they inspire a more basic question: why do we add spices to pep up meats, and not the other way around?
40 There is a biological reason for this – meat isn't spicy because meat can move. When animals are attacked, they have a wide range of options – run away, take flight, climb a tree, slither into a hole, or stand and fight. Plants, on the other hand, must stay put and endure, defending themselves (and especially their seeds) with a
45 vast array of potent chemicals.

6. Strawberry. My son announces that strawberry jam is the best thing on pancakes, and I tend to agree. I'm tempted to have another one, which is precisely how I should feel. After all, tasty fruits like berries evolved for the sole purpose of temptation, luring animals
50 like me into dispersing their precious cargo of seeds. Giving in to evolution, I eat another jam-slathered cake.

7. A Seed Bank. Cleaning up the kitchen, I tuck the flour back into a cupboard overflowing with seeds: rice, oats, almonds, walnuts, quinoa, popcorn, sesame, garbanzos, black beans, pintos, and lentils, to name
55 a few. They will keep a long time, a culinary seed bank not much different from the seeds that gather in soil, waiting for years, decades, even centuries before sprouting. Filled with seeds, clothed in seeds, and inspired by the ways we are tangled up in their rich and mysterious lives, I start my day thoroughly nourished in body and mind.

---

[19] **adorn sth./sb.** [əˈdɔːn] (fml) decorate sth./sb., make sth./sb. look beautiful

[23] **fluff** *Flaum, Fussel* **waft** (v) [wɒft] drift

[25] **flannel** [ˈflænl] piece of clothing made of thick material

[26] **spinnaker** [ˈspɪnəkə] type of sail

[30] **beverage** [ˈbevərɪdʒ] drink

[31] **flock** group or herd

[33] **herbicide** [ˈhɜːbɪsaɪd, AE: ˈɜːrbɪsaɪd] chemical used to kill unwanted plants

memory-enhancer memory booster, making it stronger

[35] **skillet** little frying pan

[36] **vine** *Kletterpflanze, Weinrebe*

[42] **take flight** run away **slither** [ˈslɪðə] slip, glide or slide

[45] **potent** [ˈpəʊtnt] powerful

[50] **disperse sth.** [dɪˈspɜːs] distribute sth. over an area

[54] **garbanzo** [gɑːˈbænzəʊ] (AE) = chickpea (BE) *Kichererbse*

pinto (AE) (here) pinto bean, type of bean

From: Orion Magazine, *July-August 2015*

Comprehension

2 Look back at the text and answer the questions below in your own
words. You may write the answers in note form.

A Why are seeds and plants so important to our everyday lives?

_____

_____

B What makes seeds so interesting for us to eat or drink?

_____

_____

C How is cotton used in our everyday lives?

_____

_____

D What theories are there about the origin of coffee?

_____

_____

E Why are all spices types of seeds or plants (and not animals)?

_____

_____

F Why are strawberries tempting?

_____

_____

Analysis

3 **a** Summarize in one or two sentences what message Thor Hanson's
enumeration '7 seeds to start your day' conveys.

b Discuss your message with a partner.

Beyond the text

4 In groups of three, discuss whether you consider the text on pp. 27–28 a list, a poem or a story. Support your view by listing characteristics for each of these text types.

> **Language help**
> aesthetic language · enumeration · pictorial representations · subjective perception of the world · narrative depiction

5 **a** Brainstorm some everyday objects that are connected to nature and have the same impact on your life as items 1–7 (pp. 27–28) have on Thor Hanson's life.

   b Writing Create a text about two of these objects in the style of Thor Hanson's enumeration.

A3 10 words technology borrowed from nature *Sue Thomas*

In another enumeration from *Orion Magazine*, Sue Thomas lists ten words that do not only refer to the natural world but also to the world of technology. Read her text and work on the tasks on pp. 32–33.

1. **Ecosystem.** The internet is often described as an ecosystem (or a sky, or a park, or a jungle), and many of its parts are named after the natural world. 'Cyberspace,' says the technology historian Fred Turner, 'is a frantic mingling of biological, digital, and frontier metaphors.'

2. **Tree.** Inside every computer, smartphone, and server is a floating forest of branching directories, all sprouting from a deeply buried 'root' folder. Open one and you'll find it connected to many others, like a leaf atop a twig that's attached, eventually, to a trunk.

3. **Spider.** One of the first search engines was named after *Lycosa kochii*, or the wolf spider. Called Lycos, the system was designed to imitate the spider's habit of catching its prey by relentless pursuit.

[6] **mingle** ['mɪŋgl] combine, mix
[13] **prey** *Beute*
relentless tireless, not giving up

4. Virus. Computer scientists have categorized two main kinds of
digital viruses. 'Zoo viruses' are those that have little chance of
spreading; often they are collected and preserved. Viruses that
exist 'in the wild' are much harder to control – some are shape-
shifters that imitate more benign forms of code, while others are
parasitic and invade computers, telephone systems, and other
networks.

[18] **benign** [bɪˈnaɪn] innocent, harmless
[26] **moth** *Motte, Nachtfalter*

5. Water. The digital world is full of watery metaphors.
We follow the Twitter stream, surf the web, listen to
torrents of music, and meet at online watering holes.
We swim in seas and oceans of data.

6. Bug. The first known computer bug was a real bug – a
moth, in fact – that got stuck inside the enormous inner
workings of an early computer in 1947. After removal,
its body was taped to a sheet of paper on which the
computer recorded its daily data, alongside the words
'first actual case of bug being found.'

7. Swarm. At Kobe University in Japan, scientists used
a swarm of forty soldier crabs to simulate the logic
function of a computer. They watched the creatures
navigate a maze, and then imitated their behavior in an
effort to improve circuit designs.

8. Worm. The first computer worm was invented by John Brunner in
his 1975 science fiction novel, *The Shockwave Rider*. He called it a
'tapeworm,' since it worked in a way similar to the fleshy parasite.
Real computer worms followed soon after.

[32] **soldier crab** *Einsiedlerkrebs*
[34] **maze** labyrinth
[35] **circuit** [ˈsɜːkɪt] *Schaltung, Schaltkreis*
[38] **tapeworm** *Bandwurm*

9. Brain. The Mandarin word for 'computer' means 'electric brain.'
Technologist Tim O'Reilly believes that hyperlinks allow the web
to grow in the same way that synapses form – but is the internet
like a brain, or is a brain like the internet?

10. Cloud. Until recently, a cloud was just a visible mass
of condensed water, but today we also imagine it as a
fog of data, accessible with a username and password,
floating somewhere above the planet. In reality, though,
it's an earthbound network of enormous computers, as
is the internet itself. The French philosopher Gaston
Bachelard once wrote that clouds – the puffy kind –
help us dream of transformation. They still do.

From: Orion Magazine, *September-October 2015*

Comprehension

1 Explain the technological meaning of the nature words below using keywords from the text on pp. 30–31.

Nature image/ metaphor	Aspect of technology
tree	*root, trunk & branches as hierarchical structures*
spider	
virus	
water	
bug	
swarm	
worm	
brain	
cloud	

Info Metaphor [ˈmetəfə] **and simile** [ˈsɪməli]
Metaphors and similes are rhetorical devices that are used to make a description more powerful. A **metaphor** is a comparison between two things (which are normally quite unlike one another) without using the words *as* or *like*. Example: *The internet is an ecosystem.*
Metaphors can make evaluations, certain ideas or connotations of the words more powerful
5 (even if sometimes unwanted). Therefore, metaphors express how we perceive the world.
Like a metaphor, a **simile** is a type of comparison. Unlike metaphors, similes use the words *like* or *as* to draw the comparison. Example: *The internet is like a brain.*

Analysis

2 Analyse the use of metaphors and similes in Sue Thomas's list of words. Examine how the natural meaning of the words is linked to the technological meaning. State if you think the choice of metaphor is fitting.

Language help
The writer uses/employs the word ... as a metaphor for ...
in order to illustrate / show / emphasize / point out ... •
I find the writer's choice/use of metaphor/simile
(un)fitting/(in)appropriate/apt/good/... because ...

Beyond the text

3 Make your own enumeration.
  a Brainstorm what is important to you and your understanding of the environment. Choose one of the following topics, or come up with your own creative alternative.

activities	books, songs, films	places and landscapes
animals and plants	...	

  b Describe what you consider important about your chosen topic. What aspects are to be included? Write a short explanation for each aspect.
  c **Writing** Compose your text. See how your idea comes across best, i.e. as a list, a poem or a narrative. Consider also the mood you want your piece of writing to have, e.g. funny or comical, explanatory, factual, sad.

A4 Our internal environment *Adam Dickinson*

Many people talk about what the 'man-made' impact on the planet is. Canadian poet Adam Dickinson (born 1974), however, asks how the environment has an impact on us, on our bodies.

Read the text below from Dickinson's poetry collection *Anatomic* and work on the tasks on p. 35.

ANATOMIC

The keys touch me when I type. My breath smells because other creatures live out their ends in my mouth. Wearing a waterproof jacket perverts my immune response. My throat is sore because of a miniature life form that, when magnified, looks like a string
5 of pearls. My neighbour's attempt to control dandelions leads to misspellings in my adrenal gland. In my lower intestine, E. coli reproduces, making vitamin K and assisting with undigested carbohydrates. My fat collects signatures from one of the most profitable companies in the world. In necessary ways and toxic
10 ways, the outside doctors the inside. This is evolutionary history and this is a metabolic response to the energy technologies of my historical moment. Petrochemicals brand hormonal messages that course through endocrine pathways and drive my metabolism. I wear multinational companies in my flesh. But I also wear symbiotic
15 and parasitic relationships with countless nonhumans who insist for their own reasons on making me human. I want to know the stories of these chemicals, metals, and organisms that compose me. I am an event, a site within which the industrial power and evolutionary pressures of my time come to write. I am a spectacular
20 and horrifying crowd. How can I read me? How can I write me? I collect my blood, urine, sweat, and feces. I send them to laboratories to determine the levels and types of chemicals and microbes I find. I get tested for hundreds of substances […]. I also tune in to the signal of my microbiome by swabbing various areas of my body for
25 bacteria – hand, genitals, ear, nose, and mouth. […] I have some initial difficulty sending this sample across the border. I am a spectacular and horrifying assemblage. I resemble a battery. I wear uranium from well water in the Canadian Shield and from the nuclear testing that marks me as a
30 child of the Cold War. I house bacterial colonies that have become empires of the Western diet, fuelled by sugar, salt, and fat. I summon the energy to write by way of metabolism already written. What is inscribed in me is in you, too.

5 **dandelion** [ˈdændɪlaɪən] *Löwenzahn*
6 **adrenal gland** [əˈdriːnl glænd] *Nebenniere*
intestine(s) [ɪnˈtestɪn] *Darm*
10 **doctor sth.** alter sth. with deceitful intention
11/13 **metabolic** [ˌmetəˈbɒlɪk]/**metabolism** [məˈtæbəlɪzəm] (connected with) all processes going on within a living body *(Stoffwechsel)*
12 **petrochemical** [ˌpetrəʊˈkemɪkl] *Erdölprodukt, Erdölchemie*
13 **endocrine** [ˈendəʊkrɪn] (adj) involving hormones
21 **feces** [ˈfiːsiːz] (pl, fml, AE) **= faeces** (BE) excrements
24 **microbiome** [ˌmaɪkrəʊˈbaɪəʊm] entirety of microbes living on or in the human body
27 **assemblage** [əˈsemblɪdʒ] (fml) collection of things, group of people

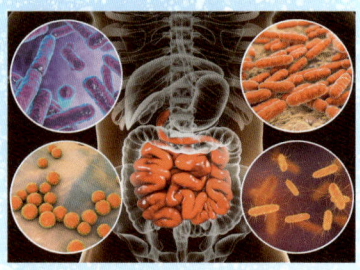

Intestinal microbiome

From: Adam Dickinson, Anatomic, *2018*

Comprehension

1 Choose whether the following statements are true or false.
   Give evidence from the text (line numbers) to prove your answer.

Statement	True	False	Evidence from text
A In many ways, the outside world has an influence inside our bodies.	○	○	line(s) _____
B Microbes live inside our bodies, but multinational industries make sure to keep chemicals out.	○	○	line(s) _____
C Our bodies are tools for the economy and industry.	○	○	line(s) _____
D What is going on inside our bodies is wonderful and terrible at the same time.	○	○	line(s) _____
E Bacteria can be controlled by eating sugar, salt and fat.	○	○	line(s) _____

Analysis

2 Comment on the style of the text. Take into account stylistic devices, syntax, word choice, stanzas, rhyme and the point of view ('Erzählperspektive').
3 Examine how the feelings of amazement and disgust are created.

Beyond the text

4 At the end of *Anatomic*, the writer claims, 'What is inscribed in me is in you, too' (ll. 33–34).
   a Decide if you agree or disagree with Dickinson's statement. Collect arguments from the text. Then work on either **b** or **c**.
   b **Speaking** Give a three-minute speech presenting your view.
   c **Writing** Write a short comment presenting your view.

Language help

from my point of view · I'm (strongly) in favour of the writer's opinion · I'm in agreement with the idea that ... · I think the writer is right/wrong when he says ... · I have to contradict the writer · I reject the idea that ... · This proves that ... · weighing the pros and cons, I come to the conclusion that ... · To sum up, ...

Part B
Demonstrating environmental awareness

Info Environmental awareness

Environmental awareness means being aware of and understanding processes of the natural environment and how they interact with different human societies and economies, with their cultures or with individual lifestyles. People cannot avoid their environmental contexts: each person will leave an environmental impact, no matter what they do. Therefore, people
5 need to realize and become aware of the relationship between humans, their activities and the environment.

To become environmentally aware, it is important to acquire knowledge and understanding of ecology and environmental issues: How is one thing connected to everything else? Acting responsibly and practising environmental awareness also means finding ways of
10 dealing with the mistakes of the past and their present consequences (climate change, industrialization, ozone layer, deforestation, pollution, depleting natural resources, using plastics/petrochemicals, etc.).

One metaphor for becoming environ-
15 mentally aware is the slogan 'go green'. In order to go green, ask yourself: How do my actions relate
20 to my environment? What impact does it have?

B1 Cry of protest *Mary and Bryan Talbot*

The comic strips on pp. 38–39 are from *Rain*, a contemporary graphic novel by British authors and illustrators Mary Talbot (born 1954) and Bryan Talbot (born 1952).

1 Take a good look at the two pages, then work on the tasks on p. 37. Before you start, find out what fracking is and why it is controversial.

Comprehension

2 Write a tweet (280 characters or less) in which you summarize your first impression of the content of the graphic novel *Rain* after having seen the two example pages A and B (on pp. 38 and 39).
Just leafed through the GN 'Rain' ...

Analysis

3 a In groups of three, choose one of the two pages (A or B) from *Rain* and analyse it. Copy the table below and complete it with your notes on the page you have chosen.

Rain	Notes on page A (p. 38) OR on page B (p. 39)
Colours and their effect	...
Style of drawing (realistic, abstract)	...
Perspective (camera angle)	...
Expression of emotions	...
Language	...
Representation of figures	...
Symbols	...

b Find a group that worked on the other page from *Rain*. Present your results and listen to the other group's results. Compare your notes.

c Discuss how the topic of protest is presented on the two pages you have looked at. Which role does language play? Find rhetorical devices that are used to express protest on the signs, e.g. metaphors (→ Info box, p. 33), puns, alliterations.

Beyond the text

4 a Work with a partner. Collect protest signs that made an impression on you. You may search on the internet or social media, or even use a sign that you have created in the past.

b Speaking Present your signs to the class and describe why they made an impression on you.

exploratory drilling *Probebohrung(en) zur Suche nach tief liegenden Lagerstätten von Gas, Erdöl oder Erdwärme* • shale gas *Schiefergas (= in Tonsteinen enthaltenes Erdgas)*

B

From: Mary and Bryan Talbot, Rain, *2019*

debt [det] sum of money a person has to pay back
climate summit official meeting between political leaders about the environment

B2 'Mercy, mercy me (The Ecology)'
Marvin Gaye

'Mercy, mercy me'

Music has always played a central role in protest movements. Some protest songs are very explicit, others might convey their message in a more subtle way.
Your teacher is going to play you a song by the US soul singer Marvin Gaye (1939–1984).

Comprehension

1 a Listening Listen to the song. While and after listening, complete the mind map below with some key words.

b Work with a partner. Compare your mind maps and discuss your impressions.

c In one sentence, summarize the message of the song.

Make sure you understand these words from the song:
– **mercury** [ˈmɜːkjəri] *Quecksilber*
– **radiation** [ˌreɪdiˈeɪʃn] *Strahlung*
– **abuse** [əˈbjuːs] *Missbrauch, Misshandlung*

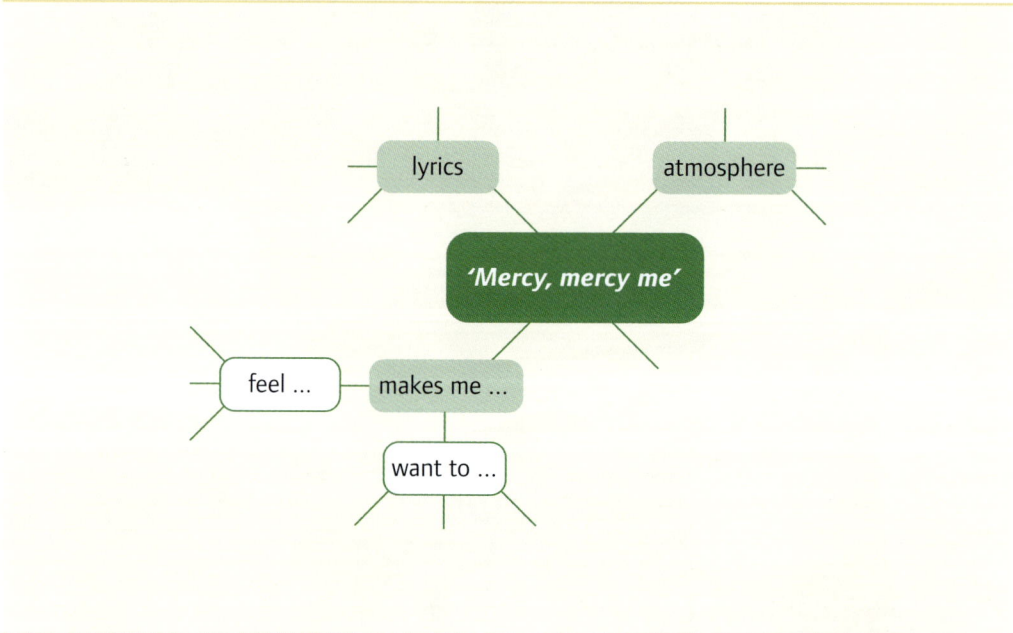

lyrics

atmosphere

'Mercy, mercy me'

feel ...

makes me ...

want to ...

Analysis

2 a Marvin Gaye's song 'Mercy, mercy me (The Ecology)' is referred to as one of the most poignant expressions of sorrow in pop music when it comes to environmental matters.
Listening Listen to the song a second time. While listening, read the lyrics your teacher is going to give you.

b Discuss the relation between the musical style of the song and its lyrics. Does the musical style help to convey the message you wrote in **1c**, or does it contradict it? → Language help, p. 41

Marvin Gaye (1939–1984)

Language help
instrumentation · slow-paced/fast-paced · catchy tune ·
melodious · associate sth. with sth. · channel sth. into sth. (= use
your energy/feelings/ideas for a particular purpose)

Beyond the text

3 **Writing** Using the results from **1** and **2**, write a review of the song
(about 250 words) in which you either agree or disagree with its
message (→ Info box).

Info Review
A review informs other people about the positive and negative aspects of a particular book,
film, song, etc. Reviews are meant to either recommend the work in question or advise
against it. Like any other essay, a review should have an **introduction**, a **middle or main
body** (including a brief summary/description that doesn't give too much away and an
evaluation of the strengths and weaknesses) and a **conclusion**.

4 Look again at the text 'Going beyond hope' in Chapter I (pp. 5–7).
In it, Derrick Jensen discusses the relation between hope and action.
Examine how Marvin Gaye's song can be related to this.

Language help
in comparison to … · in contrast to … · on the one hand, … · on the
other hand, … · whereas … · considering …, it can be said that …

5 **a** 'Mercy, Mercy me (The Ecology)' was recorded in 1971 and
published without a video. In groups of three, collect ideas of what
a video clip for the song could look like.

  b **Speaking** Present your ideas to the class.

6 **a** Work with a partner. Collect other songs that aim to raise
environmental awareness through their lyrics or video clips.

  b Prepare a two-minute presentation in which you introduce the song
and its message. Also consider the form and language of the song.

  c **Speaking** Give your presentation to the class.

Language help
convey a message · be made up of / consist of … stanzas/verses
· make use of / employ imagery/personification/alliteration/
contrast/repetition/enumeration · illustrate/emphasize/underline ·
use similes / metaphors / symbols / specific sentence structures

B3 Seeing through greenwashing

1 **a** Take a look at the two pictures below. Describe what you see.

   b State the common message of the pictures.

Info Greenwashing

In an era where most people are aware of the environmental crises, consumer industries have become particularly creative to save their businesses. Advertising and marketing campaigns that use beautiful images, metaphors or slogans to make companies appear 5 ecological on the surface have been termed 'greenwashing'.

Ten common greenwashing techniques

1. Fluffy language
   Words or terms with no clear meaning, e. g. 'eco-friendly'

2. Green products v dirty company
10 Such as efficient light bulbs made in a factory which pollutes rivers

3. Suggestive pictures
   Green images that indicate a (un-justified) green impact, e. g. flowers blooming from exhaust pipes

4. Irrelevant claims
15 Emphasizing one tiny green attribute when everything else is un-green

5. Best in class?
   Declaring you are slightly greener than the rest, even if the rest are pretty terrible

6. Just not credible
20 'Eco friendly' cigarettes anyone? 'Greening' a dangerous product doesn't make it safe

---

[7] **fluffy** (infml) light but not serious   [9] **v** (BE) = **vs** (AE) versus, against   [11] **suggestive** [səˈdʒestɪv] making you think of sth.   [13] **exhaust pipe** [ɪgˈzɔːst paɪp] *Auspuff*

7. Gobbledygook
Jargon and information that only a scientist could check or understand

8. Imaginary friends
A 'label' that looks like third-party endorsement ... except it's made up

9. No proof
It could be right, but where's the evidence?

10. Outright lying
Totally fabricated claims data

From: Selling Sustainability. Primer for Marketers. *Published by the Sustainable Lifestyles Frontier Group, 2015*

[22] **gobbledygook** ['gɒbldiguːk] (infml) complicated language that is hard to understand [25] **third-party endorsement** *unabhängige Zustimmung (von dritter Seite)* [25] **make sth. up** invent a story to trick or entertain sb. [29] **fabricate sth.** (here) invent a story in order to trick sb. [29] **claim** (n) statement without proof

Comprehension/Analysis
2 Describe in your own words what tricks are used to greenwash a product. Try to give a few examples too.

Beyond the text
3 a With a partner, discuss how words and images interact to get a (marketing or advertising) message across.
  b Examine the pros and cons of greenwashing for industries.
4 a Research 'green' terms or phrases that are found on product packaging in both English and German.
  b Complete the first two columns of the table below with the words or phrases you have found. Look up the missing English or German equivalents and add them too.
  c Use the third column to explain why the word or phrase could be misleading to consumers.

'Green' terms or phrases		
English	**German**	**Why possibly misleading?**
green	*grün*	the colour of hope and of vegetation/ photosynthesis, therefore associated with everything environmental
	umweltfreundlich	

English	German	Why possibly misleading?
organic		
	bio, Bio-	
natural		

5 In groups of three, work on either **a** or **b**.

a `Speaking` Think of an imaginary product that you want to promote. Then design an advert (verbal, visual or combined in graphics) using greenwashing techniques. Use at least six of the techniques from the list on pp. 42-43. Present your advert to the class.

b `Speaking` Design a campaign that uses words, images or graphics to make commitment to the environment attractive. Invent a creative slogan for your campaign and come up with four activities to convince people to go green. Present your ideas to the class.

6 `Mediating` You are writing for an international internet forum on 'green living'. Based on the following press release from the German Federal Ministry for Economic Cooperation and Development, write a blog entry in which you point out the reasons for the introduction of the German 'Green Button' label.

Minister Gerd Müller stellt staatliches Textilsiegel „Grüner Knopf" vor

Pressemitteilung vom 09.09.2019 | Berlin – Bundesentwicklungsminister Dr. Gerd Müller hat heute das staatliche Textilsiegel Grüner Knopf vorgestellt. Zum Start ma-
5 chen 27 Unternehmen mit. Sie haben alle die anspruchsvollen Anforderungen des Textil-siegels erfolgreich bestanden. 26 weitere Unternehmen sind derzeit im Prüfprozess.

Minister Müller: „Die Globalisierung hat
10 im 19. Jahrhundert in der Textilwirtschaft begonnen. Nun muss auch gerechte Globali-sierung in der Textilwirtschaft anfangen. Mit dem Grünen Knopf setzen wir jetzt einen hohen Standard und zeigen: Faire
15 Lieferketten sind möglich. Ab heute kann das keiner mehr in Frage stellen. Das beweisen alle Unternehmen, die mitmachen."

Produkte wie T-Shirts, Bettlaken oder Ruck-säcke müssen 26 anspruchsvolle Sozial- und
20 Umweltstandards einhalten – von Abwasser-grenzwerten und dem Verbot gefährlicher Chemikalien bis hin zu Mindestlöhnen und dem Verbot von Kinder- und Zwangs-arbeit. Zusätzlich wird das Unternehmen
25 anhand von 20 weiteren Kriterien ge-prüft: Legt es Lieferanten offen? Gibt es Beschwerdemöglichkeiten für die Näherinnen vor Ort? Schafft es Missstände ab?

Minister Müller: „Das ist das Besondere am Grünen Knopf: Das gesamte Unternehmen 30 wird kontrolliert. Einzelne Vorzeigeprodukte reichen alleine nicht aus. In dieser Tiefe prüft sonst keiner."

Zum Start deckt der Grüne Knopf die bei-den wichtigsten Arbeitsschritte „Nähen" und 35 „Färben" ab: Hier laufen alle der 100 Mil-liarden Kleidungsstücke weltweit durch. Hier arbeiten 75 Millionen Menschen. Und der Einsturz der Textilfabrik Rana Plaza [in Bangladesch am 24. April 2013] erfolgte bei 40 diesem Arbeitsschritt.

In den kommenden Jahren wird der Grüne Knopf auf weitere Produktionsschritte wie den Baumwollanbau ausgeweitet. Auch die Sozial- und Umweltkriterien werden 45 kontinuierlich weiterentwickelt, zum Bei-spiel hin zu existenzsichernden Löhnen. Ein Beirat aus Wirtschaft, Wissenschaft und Zivilgesellschaft unterstützt dies.

Minister Müller: „Fair Fashion ist ein Mega- 50 Trend. Für drei Viertel der Verbraucher ist faire Kleidung wichtig. Doch bisher fehlt die Orientierung. Mit dem Grünen Knopf ändert sich das. Mit jeder Kaufentscheidung können wir jetzt einen Beitrag leisten: Für 55 eine gerechte Globalisierung, bei der Mensch und Natur nicht für unseren Konsum ausgebeutet werden. Für Menschlichkeit und Humanität."

From: the website of www.bmz.de, *9 September 2019*

Chapter III

Learning from and about Nature

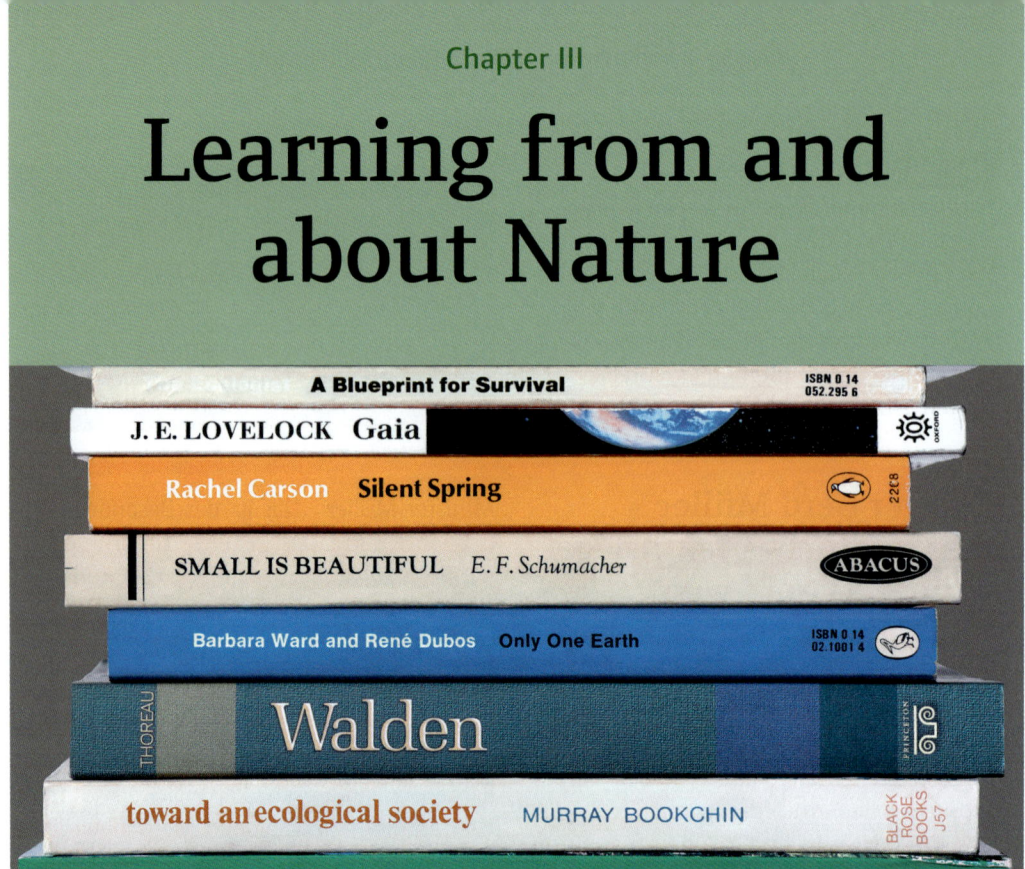

A selection of books on environmental issues, including some historic titles that have influenced the green movement

Part A
Outdoor lessons

A1 Time out in the woods *Henry David Thoreau*

Info Nature writing

Nature writing is found in many different genres but it mostly takes the form of non-fictional literature. It centres around the observation of nature. A nature writer thinks of moments with the environment, observes them very closely and describes them in larger details. The intensive experience and observation trigger a diverse range of thoughts on the
5   meaning of life and its different aspects, particularly the relationship between mankind and the non-human environment. By using the broad repertoire of literary devices, nature writers turn away from the scientific, objective descriptions of nature, favouring a more subjective description which involves the personal experience and a more individual construction of meaning.
10   Even though nature writing was developed and made popular in North America and Great Britain, it is slowly becoming more popular in Germany too.

Henry David Thoreau is regarded as the USA's earliest and most radical environmentalist. His book *Walden* ['wɔːldən] (first published in 1854 as *Walden; or, Life in the Woods*) has become one of the most beloved and widely read classics in the field of nature writing. For two years, from 1845–1847, Thoreau lived in a cabin in the woods by a lake called Walden Pond, near the city of Concord, Massachusetts, in the northeastern United States.

Henry David Thoreau (1817–1862)

Read the following excerpt from *Walden* and work on the tasks on pp. 48–49.

WALDEN.

By HENRY D THOREAU,

AUTHOR OF "A WEEK ON THE CONCORD AND MERRIMACK RIVERS."

I do not propose to write an ode to dejection, but to brag as lustily as chanticleer in the morning, standing on his roost, if only to wake my neighbors up. — Page 92.

BOSTON:
JAMES R. OSGOOD AND COMPANY,
LATE TICKNOR & FIELDS, AND FIELDS, OSGOOD, & CO.
1875.

Original title page of Walden, *with an illustration from a drawing by Thoreau's sister Sophia*

[10] **sojourner** ['sɒdʒənə] visitor or traveler
[22] **omit sth.** [ə'mɪt] leave sth. out or unmentioned
[23] **retain sth.** (rather fml) keep sth.
ego(t)ism ['iːɡəʊtɪzəm, 'eɡətɪzəm] fact of thinking you are better than others
[32] **kindred** ['kɪndrəd] (old-fashioned) your family and relatives

When I wrote the following pages, or rather the bulk of them, I lived alone, in the woods, a mile from any neighbor, in a house which I had
5 built myself, on the shore of Walden Pond, in Concord, Massachusetts, and earned my living by the labor of my hands only. I lived there two years and two months. At present
10 I am a sojourner in civilized life again. […]

Some have asked what I got to eat; if I did not feel lonesome; if I was not afraid; and the like.
15 Others have been curious to learn what portion of my income I devoted to charitable purposes; and some, who have large families, how many poor children I maintained. I will therefore ask those of my readers who
20 feel no particular interest in me to pardon me if I undertake to answer some of these questions in this book. In most books, the *I*, or first person, is omitted; in this it will be retained; that, in respect to egotism, is the main difference. We commonly do not remember that it is, after all, always
25 the first person that is speaking. I should not talk so much about myself if there were anybody else whom I knew as well. Unfortunately, I am confined to this theme by the narrowness of my experience. Moreover, I, on my side, require of every writer, first or last, a simple and sincere
30 account of his own life, and not merely what he has heard of other men's lives; some such account as he would send to his kindred from a distant land. […]

The grand necessity, then, for our bodies, is to keep warm, to keep the vital heat in us. What pains we accordingly take,

Statue of Thoreau outside the replica of his cabin near Walden Pond

35 not only with our Food, and Clothing, and Shelter, but with our beds, which are our night-clothes, robbing the nests and breasts of birds to prepare this shelter within a shelter, as the mole has its bed of grass and leaves at the end of its burrow! [...]

Most of the luxuries, and many of the so-called comforts of life, are
40 not only not indispensable, but positive hindrances to the elevation of mankind. With respect to luxuries and comforts, the wisest have ever lived a more simple and meagre life than the poor. [...]

In any weather, at any hour of the day or night, I have been anxious to improve the nick of time, and notch it on my stick too; to stand on
45 the meeting of two eternities, the past and future, which is precisely the present moment; to toe that line. [...]

To anticipate, not the sunrise and the dawn merely, but, if possible, Nature herself! How many mornings, summer and winter, before yet any neighbor was stirring about his business, have I been about mine!
50 No doubt, many of my townsmen have met me returning from this enterprise, farmers starting for Boston in the twilight, or woodchoppers going to their work. It is true, I never assisted the sun materially in his rising, but, doubt not, it was of the last importance only to be present at it. [...]

55 In short, I am convinced, both by faith and experience, that to maintain one's self on this earth is not a hardship but a pastime, if we will live simply and wisely; as the pursuits of the simpler nations are still the sports of the more artificial. [...]

From: Henry David Thoreau, Walden; or, Life in the Woods, *1854/1995*

37 mole *Maulwurf*
38 burrow hole in the ground used for shelter
40 indispensable *unent-behrlich*
hindrance to sth. ['hɪndrəns] thing or person that holds sth. back
elevation (fml) giving sb. higher status or a more important position
42 meagre ['miːgə] sparse, poor, slim
44 the nick of time (hier) *der gegebene Augen-blick*
notch sth. cut a V-shaped mark into sth.
45 eternity *Ewigkeit*
46 toe the line *sich in einer (Start-)Linie zu einem Wettlauf auf-stellen;* (hier) *sich fügen, bereit sein*
56 pastime activity that you enjoy doing in your free time
57 pursuit [pə'sjuːt] (here) activity, hobby
58 artificial [ˌɑːtɪ'fɪʃl] (here) cultured

Comprehension

1 Sum up in your own words what the narrator says about:
  – his living situation,
  – the 'luxuries' of life.

2 Work with a partner. In your own words, rephrase the author's explanation of the role of the 'I' in his text (ll. 22 ff.).

Analysis

3 Refer back to **2**. Discuss why the first-person speaker is important in this context.

4 Thoreau's *Walden* is referred to as an essential work of nature writing (→ Info box, p. 46). Look at the excerpt again:
  – Explain which values are given priority and which ones are omitted.
  – Point out how the writer puts the environment and environmental living at the forefront.

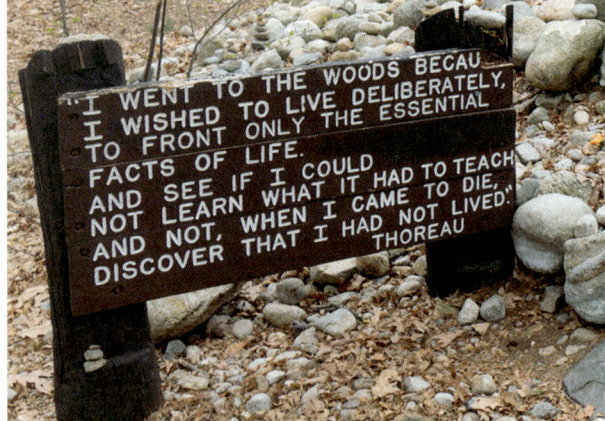

Famous Thoreau quote near his cabin site at Walden Pond

Beyond the text

5 `Writing` Write a creative non-fiction text about a place that you like
or find interesting. Choose one of the following types of text: a blog
entry, an open letter to a general audience, an article for a school
magazine or an essay. Before you start writing, 'explore' your place
and think about your writing task by following the eight steps below.

1. Choose your place and imagine you are there. Sit down, close your
   eyes, take a deep breath and 'take the place in'.
2. In your imagination, open your eyes and start taking notes.
   Describe what you see: look from different angles, zoom in and
   out, look down. Describe how these visual aspects go together.
3. Pay attention to the rest of your body. Describe all the other ways
   you can sense the place, e. g. touch, taste, listen and smell.
4. Reflect on how you feel about this place. What emotions or
   memories does it hold for you? How is it linked to your own
   identity?
5. Examine what human events happened at the place: Who lived
   there, and how? Who owns or controls the place? Has it been tied
   to events happening elsewhere, through commerce or politics?
   Has anyone made art, music or written about it? What have
   humans done to preserve the place? What have they done that
   has hurt the place (e. g. pollution, warfare, habitat loss, climate
   change)?
6. Consider who or what is sharing the place with you: people,
   plants, animals, birds, insects, etc. What kinds of life do all these
   creatures have there? Is there anything that you cannot see?
7. Speculate how the place is without you there: How long has the
   place been the way it is now? What was it like a hundred years
   ago? What might it be like a hundred years from now?
8. Comment on the relevance of this place: Is it a place of
   importance? What would be lost if it was destroyed tomorrow?
   Can we learn or be wiser from this place?

EXTRA: Reflect on the impact this writing task has on you:

- What happens when you observe, perceive, think and write about
  your place?
- Which parts of the writing task were easier, which ones were
  harder, and why?
- During which step have you taken the most and the least notes?
  Is there a correlation?
- Why did you choose this specific place?
- What would change if you focused on a different place?
- How could you help others to see or understand your place from
  your perspective?

A2 Teaching about the environment *Barry Lopez*

Barry Lopez (born 1945) is one of the USA's outstanding contemporary nature writers. His work is widely read. In the following excerpt, he reflects on how to teach about the environment and inspire others to enjoy a walk in the woods.

Read the text and work on the tasks on pp. 51–53.

[…] My wife and I do not have children, but children we know, or children whose parents we're close to, are
5 often here. They always want to go into the woods. And I wonder what to tell them.

In the beginning, years ago, I think I said too much.
10 I spoke with an encyclopedic knowledge of the names of plants or the names of

birds passing through in season. Gradually I came to say less. After a while the only words I spoke, beyond answering a question or calling
15 attention quickly to the slight difference between a sprig of red cedar and a sprig of incense cedar, were to elucidate single objects.

I remember once finding a fragment of a raccoon's jaw in an alder thicket. I sat down alongside the two children with me and encouraged them to find out who this was – with only the three teeth still intact
20 in a piece of the animal's maxilla to guide them. The teeth told by their shape and placement what this animal ate. By a kind of visual extrapolation its size became clear. There were other clues, immediately present, which told, with what I could add of climate and terrain, how this animal lived, how its broken jaw came to be lying here. Raccoon,
25 they surmised. And tiny tooth marks along the bone's broken edge told of a mouse's hunger for calcium.

We set the jaw back and went on.

If I had known more
30 about raccoons, finer points of osteology, we might have guessed more: say, whether it was male or female. But what we deduced was all
35 we needed. Hours later, the maxilla, lost behind us in the

The skull of a dead raccoon

---

15 **sprig** twig on a tree
16 **elucidate sth.** [ɪˈluːsɪdeɪt] (fml) explain sth. or make sth. clearer
17 **rac(c)oon** [rəˈkuːn] *Waschbär*
jaw (Unter-, Ober-) *Kiefer*
alder [ˈɔːldə] *Erle*
20 **maxilla** [mækˈsɪlə] upper jaw
22 **extrapolation** [ɪkˌstræpəˈleɪʃn] (fml) process of using known information to guess what might happen
25 **surmise** [səˈmaɪz] (fml) guess, suppose
31 **osteology** [ˌɒstiˈɒlədʒi] anatomy of bones
34 **deduce sth.** [dɪˈdjuːs] (fml) form a reasonable opinion about sth. after considering known facts

detritus of the forest floor, continued to effervesce. It was tied faintly to all else we spoke of that afternoon.

In speaking with children who might one day take a permanent
40 interest in natural history – as writers, as scientists, as filmmakers, as anthropologists – I have sensed that an extrapolation from a single fragment of the whole is the most invigorating experience I can share with them. I think children know that nearly anyone can learn the names of things; the impression made on them on this level is fleeting.
45 What takes a lifetime to learn, they comprehend, is the existence and substance of myriad relationships: it is these relationships, not the things themselves, that ultimately hold the human imagination.

The brightest children, it has often struck me, are fascinated by metaphor – with what is shown in the set of relationships bearing on
50 the raccoon, for example, to lie quite beyond the raccoon. In the end, you are trying to make clear to them that everything found at the edge of one's senses – the high note of the winter wren, the thick perfume of propolis that drifts downwind from spring willows, the brightness of wood chips scattered by beaver – that all this fits together. The
55 indestructibility of these associations conveys a sense of permanence that nurtures the heart, that cripples one of the most insidious of human anxieties, the one that says, you do not belong here, you are unnecessary. […]

The quickest door to open in the woods for a child is the one
60 that leads to the smallest room, by knowing the name each thing is called. The door […] is marked by a hesitancy to speak at all, rather to encourage by example a sharpness of the senses. If one speaks it should only be to say, as well as one can, how wonderfully all this fits together, to indicate what a long, fierce peace can derive from this
65 knowledge.

From: Barry Holstun Lopez, Crossing Open Ground, 1988

37 detritus [dɪ'traɪtəs] (fml) waste made of organic matter
effervesce [ˌefə'ves] *sprudeln, schäumen; hier: jdn. gedanklich beschäftigen*
faintly a little bit
41 anthropologist [ˌænθrə'pɒlədʒɪst] researcher of human cultures and ways of life
42 invigorating [ɪn'vɪgəreɪtɪŋ] (adj) stimulating
46 myriad ['mɪriəd] (adj, literary) very large in number
52 wren [ren] *Zaunkönig (Vogelart)*
53 propolis ['prɒpəlɪs] *Propolis (Wabenbaustoff der Bienen)*
willow *Weide(nbaum)*
55 indestructability [ˌɪndɪˌstrʌktə'bɪləti] fact that sth. is impossible to destroy or break
56 cripple sth. *etw. lahmlegen, etw. schwächen*
insidious [ɪn'sɪdiəs] (fml) *heimtückisch, hinterhältig*
61 hesitancy *Zögerlichkeit, Zurückhaltung*
64 fierce [fɪəs] extremely powerful

Comprehension

1 Barry Lopez mentions in his text that he has used two different approaches to share knowledge and pass on environmental awareness to children. The first approach could be called 'the encyclopedic approach'. Look back at the text to find out what alternative approach Barry Lopez has used. Think of a name for it and add it at the top of the right column in the table on the following page (p. 52). Then complete the table by listing the main features of each approach.

Encyclopedic approach	_____ approach

Analysis

2 Examine the perspective of the speaker in the text on pp. 50–51.

3 Speculate about the audience (target group) of the text. Who might it be written for?

Beyond the text

4 **a** Give an example of your own learning experience with each of the two approaches from **1**.

   b With a partner, compare the features and examples of both approaches. Which points do you agree or disagree on? Do you have examples in common?

5 **a** Comment on the statement below. Refer to the text and give examples to support your argumentation.

   Nature experience and access to nature are a human right and should therefore be a part of education in school.

   b Prepare a brief speech to your peers in which you present your arguments from **a**.

   c Speaking In groups of 4–5, give your speech.

   d Listen to the other group members' speeches and give each other feedback.

Language help

Upon first reading …, I thought … · … reminds me of … · I associate … with … · … cannot be expected to … · It must be taken into account that … · On the one hand, … · On the other hand, … · In my experience … · I feel like … · It seems to be true that … · I have the impression that … · I would presume that …

6 a Describe the cartoon on the right.

www.CartoonStock.com

> **Language help**
> forest · deforestation · rainforest ·
> cut down trees · carbon dioxide [daɪˈɒksaɪd] ·
> logger · logging

b Analyse the cartoon. Comment on its message.

c Share your results. Compare and discuss the different messages.

d Relate the cartoon to the text by Barry Lopez on pp. 50–51.

A3 The stench of dead matter
Helon Habila

stench unpleasant smell

The novel *Oil on Water* by Helon Habila (born 1967) focuses on Nigeria and its oil industry. While looking for the kidnapped wife of a European oil executive in the Niger Delta, the young journalist Rufus and his colleague Zaq experience how the interests of corrupt governments, international oil companies and militant groups have transformed former fishing grounds and communities.

NIGERIA
AFRICA MAP

1 a Before reading the novel excerpt on pp. 54–55 and working on the tasks on pp. 55–58, look at the photo below and describe it (→ Language help).

b Point out what associations the photo evokes for you.

c Find a suitable title.

> **Language help**
> in the foreground/background ·
> in the middle/centre · on the
> left/right · the situation
> reminds me of … · the picture
> addresses the topic/issue
> of … · the photo reveals … ·
> the atmosphere created by
> the black colours is … ·
> it is likely/probable that … ·
> the photo makes me feel …

– Who lives here?

The old man shrugged. – Nobody.

– Where did the people go?

– Dem left because of too much fighting.

5 The village looked as if a deadly epidemic had swept through it.

A square concrete platform dominated the village centre like some sacrificial altar. Abandoned oil-drilling paraphernalia was strewn around the platform; some appeared to be sprouting out of widening cracks in the concrete, alongside thick clumps of grass. High up in the

10 rusty rigging wasps flew in and out of their nests. A weather-beaten signboard near the platform said: oil well no. 2. 1999. 15,000 houses began not too far away from the derelict platform. We went from one squat brick structure to the next, from compound to compound, but they were all empty, with wide-open windows askew on broken hinges,

15 while overhead the roofs had big holes through which strong sunlight fell. Behind one of the houses we found a chicken pen with about ten chickens inside, all dead and decomposing, the maggots trafficking beneath the feathers. We covered our noses and moved on to the next compound, but it wasn't much different: cooking pots stood open

20 and empty on cold hearths; next to them stood water pots filled with water on whose surface mosquito larvae thickly flourished. It took less than an hour to traverse the little village, going from one deserted household to the next, taking pictures, hoping to meet perhaps one accidental straggler, one survivor, one voice to interview.

25 We left. Zaq looked as if he was about to throw up, his face was sweaty, and he raised the bottle to his lips many times before the alertness returned to his eyes. We often stopped to rest, and the river grew narrower each time we set out again. Soon we were in a dense mangrove swamp; the water underneath us had turned foul

30 and sulphurous; insects rose from the surface in swarms to settle in a mobile cloud above us, biting our arms and faces and ears. The boy and the old man appeared to be oblivious to the insects; they kept their eyes narrowed, focused on burrowing the boat through the gnarled, hanging roots that grew out of the water like proboscis gasping for

35 air. The atmosphere grew heavy with the suspended stench of dead matter. We followed a bend in the river and in front of us we saw dead birds draped over tree branches, their outstretched wings black and slick with oil; dead fishes bobbed white-bellied between tree roots.

The next village was almost a replica of the last: the same empty

40 squat dwellings, the same ripe and flagrant stench, the barrenness, the oil slick, and the same indefinable sadness in the air, as if a community of ghosts were suspended above the punctured zinc roofs, unwilling to depart, yet powerless to return. In the village centre we found the communal well. Eager for a drink, I bent under the wet, mossy pivotal

45 beam and peered into the well's blackness, but a rank smell wafted from

---

7 paraphernalia [ˌpærəfəˈneɪliə] (uncountable) articles of equipment

8 sprout grow

10 rigging (here) structure

12 derelict [ˈderəlɪkt] left by everyone

13 squat [skwɒt] low
compound [ˈkɒmpaʊnd] (n) (here) closed-off area with a group of buildings

14 askew [əˈskjuː] (adj) open
hinge [hɪndʒ] piece of metal a door or window is attached to so that it can be opened

17 maggot [ˈmægət] *Made*

22 traverse sth. [trəˈvɜːs] move through sth.

24 straggler *Nachzügler/ -in*

25 throw up (infml) be sick

30 sulphurous [ˈsʌlfərəs] containing sulphur *(Schwefel)* or smelling of sulphur

32 oblivious to sth. [əˈblɪvɪəs] unaware of sth.

33 burrow sth. through sth. (here) push sth. through sth.
gnarled [nɑːld] twisted

34 proboscis [prəˈbɒsɪs], pl: **probosces** [prəˈbɒsiːz]: long nose (e. g. of an elephant)

39 replica [ˈreplɪkə] (n) copy

40 flagrant [ˈfleɪgrənt] (here) clearly obvious
barrenness fact of soil not having good quality to grow plants

42 puncture sth. [ˈpʌŋktʃə] make a hole in sth.

45 rank (adj) (here) smelling bad
waft [wɒft] (v) float

its hot depths and slapped my face; I reeled away, my head aching from the encounter. Something organic, perhaps
50 human, lay dead and decomposing down there, its stench mixed with that unmistakable smell of oil. At the other end of the village a little river
55 trickled towards the big river where we had left our boat. The patch of grass growing by the water was suffocated by a film of oil, each blade covered
60 with blotches like the liver spots on a smoker's hands.

Warning sign along the Nembe creek in Nigeria's oil state of Bayelsa

We felt drained just standing there, and so we left. We pushed the boat into deeper
65 water and scrambled in. By now Zaq seemed to have lost even the energy – and the will – to lift the bottle to his mouth; it lay neglected by his feet, the piss-coloured liquid in it sloshing back and forth with the movement of the boat. He sat with his hands spread
70 wide on either side of his seat, holding on for dear life, and with each motion of the boat I waited for the vomit to come spewing out of his mouth, but somehow he kept it down.

– Do you want to stop at the next village?

– No, no more villages.

From: Helon Habila, Oil on Water, *2011*

47 **reel** *taumeln*
55 **trickle** (of liquid) flow slowly in a thin line
58 **suffocate sth.** ['sʌfəkeɪt] make sth. die by not giving it enough oxygen
60 **blotch** *Fleck*
68 **slosh** (of liquid) move back and forth

Info Ecocriticism

Ecocriticism is a relatively new field of literary study that examines how nature and the natural world are imagined through literary texts. It considers the relationship that humans have with their non-human environment and focuses on both 'natural' and 'human-built' environments. An ecocritical reading can be applied to any text, song, picture or object even if it is not (explicitly) concerned with environmental awareness.

Comprehension

2 In your own words, describe the condition of the village.

3 Explain why Rufus doesn't want to see more villages.

4 Work with a partner. Find 3–5 adjectives to describe the atmosphere of the scene.

Analysis

> **Info Atmosphere** ['ætməsfɪə]
> Atmosphere is the feeling or mood created by an author in their work. The setting, use of language and characterization all contribute to the atmosphere of a work.

5 a Work with a partner. Analyse how atmosphere is created in the excerpt from *Oil on Water* (pp. 54–55). Examine how language is used to evoke certain images and feelings. Give the meaning of the quotes in the table below and add the image or feeling associated with them.

Quote	Meaning	Image/Feeling
'… as if a deadly epidemic had swept through it.' (l. 5)	*no living being in the village*	
'… sacrificial altar.' (l. 7)		
'Abandoned oil-drilling paraphernalia was strewn around … cracks in the concrete … weather-beaten signboard …' (ll. 7–11)		
'… wide-open windows askew on broken hinges …' (l. 14)		

Quote	Meaning	Image/Feeling
'… all dead and decomposing, the maggots trafficking beneath the feathers.' (ll. 17–18)		
'… cooking pots stood open and empty on cold hearths …' (ll. 19–20)		
'… water on whose surface mosquito larvae thickly flourished.' (l. 21)		
'… hoping to meet perhaps one accidental straggler, one survivor, one voice to interview.' (ll. 23–24)		
'… the water underneath us had turned foul and sulphurous; insects rose from the surface in swarms to settle in a mobile cloud above us, biting our arms and faces and ears.' (ll. 29–31)		
'… dead birds draped over tree branches, their outstretched wings black and slick with oil; dead fishes bobbed white-bellied between tree roots.' (ll. 36–38)		

Quote	Meaning	Image/Feeling
'… a community of ghosts were suspended above the punctured zinc roofs, unwilling to depart, yet powerless to return.' (ll. 41–43)		
'The patch of grass growing by the water was suffocated by a film of oil …' (ll. 57–59)		

5 b Discuss narrative techniques, the syntax, the word fields and the stylistic devices used in the text. Do they evoke certain images and feelings? Write notes in the table below.

Narrative technique(s) and effect(s)	
Syntax and word fields	
Stylistic devices	

Beyond the text

6 a In groups of three, do some research on the oil industry in Nigeria. Focus on the different stakeholders as well as the ecological and social consequences for the country.

b Prepare a two-minute presentation in which you present your findings.

c Speaking Give the presentation and discuss your results in class. Write down facts that are new to you.

Part B
Scientific literature – literary science

B1 A fable for tomorrow *Rachel Carson*

Rachel Carson was a trained marine biologist who later turned to nature writing. In her book *Silent Spring* (1962), she wrote about the impact of pesticide on the US public. The book brought much opposition, especially from politicians and the chemical industry. But it became a huge international success and propelled the US environmental movement forward.

Read the introductory Chapter I from *Silent Spring* and work on the tasks on pp. 61–62.

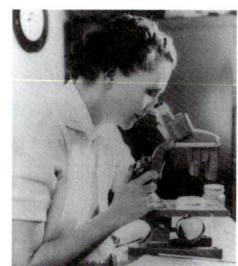

Rachel Carson (1907–1964)

There was once a town in the heart of America where all life seemed to live in harmony with its surroundings. The town lay in the midst of a checkerboard of prosperous farms, with fields of grain and hillsides of orchards where, in spring, white clouds of bloom drifted above the
5 green fields. In autumn, oak and maple and birch set up a blaze of colour that flamed and flickered across a backdrop of pines. The foxes barked in the hills and deer silently crossed the fields, half hidden in the mists of the autumn mornings.

Along the roads, laurel, viburnum and alder, great ferns and
10 wildflowers delighted the traveller's eye through much of the year. Even in winter the roadsides were places of beauty, where countless birds came to feed on the berries and on the seed heads of the dried weeds rising above the snow. The countryside was, in fact, famous for the abundance and variety of its bird life, and when the flood of migrants
15 was pouring through in spring and autumn people travelled from great distances to observe them. Others came to fish the
20 streams, which flowed clear and cold out of the hills and contained shady pools where trout lay. So it had been from the days many
25 years ago when the first settlers raised their houses, sank their wells, and built their barns.

³ **checkerboard** *Schachbrett*
prosperous [ˈprɒspərəs] (fml) economically successful and powerful
⁴ **orchard** [ˈɔːtʃəd] land with numerous fruit or nut trees
⁵ **oak** *Eiche*
maple *Ahorn*
birch *Birke*
⁶ **pine** *Kiefer, Pinie*
⁹ **laurel** [ˈlɒrəl] *Lorbeerbaum*
viburnum [vaɪˈbɜːnəm] *Schneeballstrauch*
alder [ˈɔːldə] *Erle*
²³ **trout** *Forelle(n)*

Then a strange blight crept over the area and everything began to
30 change. Some evil spell had settled on the community: mysterious
maladies swept the flocks of chickens; the cattle and sheep sickened
and died. Everywhere was a shadow of death. The farmers spoke of
much illness among their families. In the town the doctors had become
more and more puzzled by new kinds of sickness appearing among
35 their patients. There had been several sudden and unexplained deaths,
not only among adults but even among children, who would be stricken
suddenly while at play and die within a few hours.

There was a strange stillness. The birds, for example – where had
they gone? Many people spoke of them, puzzled and disturbed. The
40 feeding stations in the backyards were deserted. The few birds seen
anywhere were moribund; they trembled violently and could not fly. It
was a spring without voices. On the mornings that had once throbbed
with the dawn chorus of robins, catbirds, doves, jays, wrens, and
scores of other bird voices there was now no sound; only silence lay
45 over the fields and woods and marsh.

On the farms the hens brooded, but no chicks hatched. The farmers
complained that they were unable to raise any pigs – the litters were
small and the young survived only a few days. The apple trees were
coming into bloom but no bees droned among the blossoms, so there
50 was no pollination and there would be no fruit.

The roadsides, once so attractive, were now lined with browned and
withered vegetation as though swept by fire. These, too, were silent,
deserted by all living things. Even the streams were now lifeless.
Anglers no longer visited them, for all the fish had died.
55 In the gutters under the eaves and between the shingles
of the roofs, a white granular powder still showed a few
patches; some weeks before it had fallen like snow upon
the roofs and the lawns, the fields and streams.

No witchcraft, no enemy action had silenced the rebirth
60 of new life in this stricken world. The people had done it
themselves.

This town does not actually exist, but it might easily have a
thousand counterparts in America or elsewhere in the world. I know of
no community that has experienced all the misfortunes I describe. Yet
65 every one of these disasters has actually happened somewhere, and
many real communities have already suffered a substantial number of
them. A grim spectre has crept upon us almost unnoticed, and this
imagined tragedy may easily become a stark reality we all shall know.

What has already silenced the voices of spring in countless towns in
70 America? This book is an attempt to explain.

From: Rachel Carson, Silent Spring, *1962*

---

29 **blight** *Mehltau, Plage*
31 **flock** group of birds
41 **moribund** ['mɒrɪbʌnd]
(fml) dying
42 **throb** vibrate or beat
43 **robin** ['rɒbɪn]
Rotkehlchen
catbird *Katzendrossel*
jay *Eichelhäher*
wren [ren] *Zaunkönig*
44 **scores of** many,
numerous
46 **brood** (of birds) sit on
eggs until the young
come out of them
46 **hatch** (of a young bird)
come out of the egg
49 **drone** (v) buzz and
hum
55 **eaves** (n, pl) lower
edges of a roof that
stick out beyond the
walls
shingle ['ʃɪŋgl] *Schindel
(zum Decken des
Daches)*
67 **grim** (adj) mean,
gloomy
spectre ['spektə] ghost,
spirit

Comprehension

1 Using information from the text, complete the following sentences in your own words.

ll. 2–6: The town lay _____

_____

ll. 10–13: Even in winter _____

_____

ll. 13–18: The countryside was famous for _____

_____

ll. 30–32: Some evil spell _____

_____

ll. 40–41: The few birds seen were _____

_____

ll. 51–52: The roadsides were _____

_____

Analysis

2 Explain the title of the book *(Silent Spring)*. What has caused the silence?

3 Analyse the beginning of the excerpt (ll. 1–8). Pay special attention to the narrative elements used (e.g. from a fairy tale) and explain their function.

4 Examine the description of nature in the text. What features are described and how? What effect could this have on the audience?

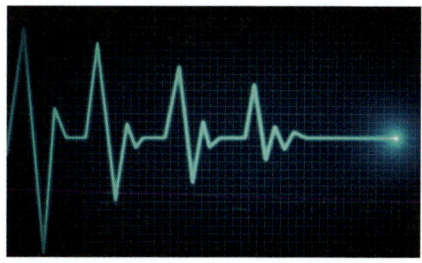

Language help
variety of wildlife · diversity of wildflowers, birds and weeds · mass extinction · overfishing · illness and death of different species

Beyond the text

5 Assess whether Rachel Carson's text is still relevant today or not.

6 a Explore the virtual exhibition on the story of the book *Silent Spring*. The webcode on the right will lead you to the exhibition.

  b While exploring the virtual exhibition, collect information on one of the following aspects:
- – the legacy and heritage of *Silent Spring*
- – *Silent Spring* in popular culture
- – *Silent Spring* in literature and the arts

  c Prepare a short statement presenting the information that you have collected.

  d `Speaking` Give the presentation to the class.

> Virtual exhibition:
> 📄 ⊙ **cornelsen.de**
> ➕ 🔊 **Code: wepefa**

B2 It's all just weather *Jonathan Safran Foer*

Some people who reject scientific evidence also reject the fact that human activity is warming our planet at alarming rates. Others believe the facts but fail to make the necessary changes – a dilemma that Jonathan Safran Foer (born 1977) is examining in his book *We are the Weather. Saving the Planet Begins at Breakfast* (2019).

Read the following excerpt from the book and work on the tasks on p. 64.

There is a place at which one's personal business and the business of being one of seven billion earthlings intersect. And for perhaps the first moment in history, the expression 'one's time' makes little sense. Climate change is not a jigsaw puzzle on the coffee table, which can
5 be returned to when the schedule allows and the feeling inspires. It is a house on fire. The longer we fail to take care of it, the harder it becomes to take care of, and because of positive feedback loops – white ice melting to dark water that absorbs more heat; thawing permafrost releasing huge amounts of methane, one of the worst greenhouse gases
10 – we will very soon reach a tipping point of 'runaway climate change,' when we will be unable to save ourselves, no matter our efforts.

² **intersect** [ˌɪntəˈsekt] meet, cross each other
⁷ **positive feedback loop** *positive Rückkopplungs-schleife*
⁸ **thaw** [θɔː] melt

We do not have the luxury of living in our time. We cannot go about our lives as if they were only ours. In a way that was not true for our ancestors, the lives we live will create a future that cannot be undone.
15 Imagine if history were such that if Lincoln hadn't abolished slavery in 1863, then America would be condemned to uphold the institution of slavery for the rest of time. [...]

There are several pivotal moments in the Bible when God asks people where they are. The two most cited instances are when he
20 finds Adam hiding after eating the forbidden fruit and says 'Where are you?,' and when he calls to Abraham before asking him to sacrifice his only son. Clearly an omniscient God knows where his creations are. His questions are not about the location of a body in space but about the location of a self within a person.

25 We have our own modern version of this. When we think back on moments when history seemed to happen before our eyes – Pearl Harbor, the assassination of John F. Kennedy, the fall of the Berlin Wall, September 11 – our reflex is to ask others where they were when it happened. Yet as with God in the Bible, we are not really trying
30 to establish someone's coordinates. We are asking something deeper about their connection to the moment, with the hope of situating our own.

The word 'crisis' derives from the Greek *krisis*, meaning 'decision.'

The environmental crisis, though a universal experience, doesn't
35 feel like an event that we are a part of. It doesn't feel like an event at all. And despite the trauma of a hurricane, wildfire, famine, or extinction, it's unlikely that a weather event will inspire a 'Where were you when ...' question of anyone who didn't live through it – perhaps not even of those who did live through it. It's all just weather. Just
40 environmental.

But future generations will almost certainly look back and wonder where we were in the biblical sense: Where was our selfhood? What decisions did the crisis inspire? Why on earth – why on *Earth* – did we choose our suicide and their sacrifice?

45 Perhaps we could plead that the decision wasn't ours to make: as much as we cared, there was nothing we could do. We didn't know enough at the time. Being mere individuals, we didn't have the means to enact consequential change. We didn't run the oil companies. We weren't making government policy. Perhaps we could argue, as Roy
50 Scranton does in his *New York Times* essay 'Raising My Child in a Doomed World,' that 'we [were] not free to choose how we live[d] any more than we [were] free to break the laws of physics.' The ability to save ourselves, and save them, was not in our hands.

But that would be a lie.

From: Jonathan Safran Foer, We are the Weather. Saving the Planet Begins at Breakfast, *2019*

12 **go about sth.** deal with sth.
14 **ancestor** ['ænsestə] family member who lived a long time ago
15 **Abraham Lincoln** ['lɪŋkən] (1809–1865), President of the USA (1861–1865)
16 **be condemned to do sth.** [kən'demd] be forced to do sth. unpleasant
18 **pivotal** ['pɪvətl] (adj) very important
19 **cite sth.** quote sth.
21 **sacrifice sb.** ['sækrɪfaɪs] *jdn. opfern*
22 **omniscient** [ɒm'nɪsiənt] (adj) knowing everything
26 **Pearl Harbor** US harbo(u)r on the island of Oahu, Hawaii; attacked by Japan on 7 December 1941, which caused the USA to take part in World War II
27 **assassination** [əˌsæsɪ'neɪʃn] murder of an important person, especially for political reasons
John F. Kennedy (1917–1963), President of the USA (1961–1963)
28 **September 11** date of a series of coordinated suicide airplane attacks in the USA which killed 2977 people. Two airplanes crashed into the World Trade Center in New York City.
36 **famine** ['fæmɪn] lack of food
42 **selfhood** personality
45 **plead** ask sb. for sth. in a very strong way
47 **mere** (adj) used to emphasize how unimportant sth. or sb. is
the means (n, pl) *die Mittel*
48 **enact sth.** [ɪ'nækt] put sth. into practice

Comprehension

1 Summarize the text in no more than 150 words.
2 State the main message of Safran Foer's text in one sentence.

> ### Language help
> argue · state · point out · claim · believe · think · explain · criticize · suggest · doubt · compare X to Y · use examples to confirm/prove that … · agree/disagree with the view that … · try to convince the readers that … · conclude

Climate change protest in London, September 2019

Analysis

3 Analyse how the author conveys his message. Focus on the use of language and stylistic devices.
4 Examine the tone of the text (→ Info box). Choose at least two adjectives from the Language help box to describe it. Explain your choice.

> ### Info Tone
> The tone of a text is the expression (direct or not) of how a writer feels about their topic. It not only reveals an author's attitude towards a topic, but also how they feel about the reader(s). Elements such as diction (i. e. choice of words), syntax, speaker and imagery can influence the tone of a text.

> ### Language help
> detached · ironic · angry · distanced · serious · humorous · solemn · intimate · playful · concerned · hopeful · sarcastic · provocative · visionary · polemic · thoughtful · satiric · neutral · informal

Beyond the text

5 Writing Imagine that you have your own youth blog about the environment. Write a blog post in which you explain the contradiction between the original meaning of *crisis* (l. 33) and the perception of the climate crisis as 'just weather' (l. 39).

B3 Preserving what's precious: John Muir and Yosemite

In Chapter I (A2, p. 10) you read about John Muir, a key figure of the early environmental movement. The following podcast introduces you to his poetic writings on nature and his lifelong commitment to preserving the wilderness he admired.

Podcast online:
📖 ▶ cornelsen.de
➕ 🔊 Code: ririvi

US President Theodore Roosevelt (1858–1919) and naturalist John Muir (1838–1914) standing on Glacier Point in Yosemite [jəʊˈsemət i] Valley, California, during a camping trip in 1903

Make sure you understand these words and phrases from the podcast:
– federal land preservation
– breadth
– change the face of conservation
– easy of access
– hospitable [hɒˈspɪtəbl, ˈhɒspɪtəbl]
– rugged [ˈrʌgɪd]
– enchanted
– from base to summit
– slope
– (profound) solitude
– majestic operations of nature
– reveal sth.
– carved

Comprehension

1 a `Listening` Listen to the podcast. While listening, write down at least three keywords that sum up Muir's description of nature.

b `Listening` Listen to the podcast again and tick the correct sentence endings.

1 With his writings, John Muir taught his readers about the importance of experiencing and protecting ...
- **A** California.
- **B** the Yosemite region.
- **C** nature and the environment.
- **D** the natural habitat of animals.

2 Muir describes the weather in the Sierra Nevada as mostly ...
- **A** sunny with few storms.
- **B** cloudy with few storms.
- **C** cloudy with many storms.
- **D** sunny with strong, beautiful storms.

3 The Yosemite National Park is a central section of the Sierra Nevada, which is ...
- **A** 36 miles long and 48 miles wide.
- **B** 63 miles long and 84 miles wide.
- **C** 84 miles long and 63 miles wide.
- **D** 48 miles long and 36 miles wide.

4 Muir describes the glaciers as being the sculptors of ...
- **A** lakes and rivers.
- **B** lakes and icebergs.
- **C** forests and rivers.
- **D** forests and icebergs.

5 Muir wrote that the Sierra should not be called the Nevada or Snowy Range but the …
- **A** White Range.
- **B** Range of Light.
- **C** Range of Beautiful Light.
- **D** Range of Natural Beauty.

6 Upon finding living glaciers, Muir came up with the theory that …
- **A** the glaciers needed to be protected.
- **B** the Yosemite Valley was discovered fifty years before.
- **C** the shape of the Yosemite Valley was originally sculpted by them.
- **D** the shape of the Yosemite Valley was going to be sculpted by glaciers for years to come.

7 When President Roosevelt toured around the country and some of its most beautiful landscapes, he …
- **A** wrote his first book about the experience.
- **B** contacted Muir and asked him to support his campaign.
- **C** contacted Muir and asked him to take him to Yosemite.
- **D** contacted Muir and asked him to take him to Yellowstone.

8 Muir used Roosevelt's visit to …
- **A** convince him to give financial support.
- **B** have the country's most powerful man openly support Yosemite.
- **C** gain political experience by being around a very powerful person.
- **D** gain political experience by joining Roosevelt in his political endeavours.

Beyond the text

2 John Muir is not only famous for his work as an environmentalist, but also for his writings that reflect the beauty of nature and express his admiration for it. Work on either **a** or **b**.

a `Speaking` Work in groups of three. With the help of different sources, find out more about John Muir. Present the results of your research.

b `Speaking` Prepare and record your own podcast (five minutes maximum) in which you talk about your connection with nature. Present your podcast to the class.

Chapter IV
The Art of Saving the Planet

Part A
Communicating environmental facts

A1 A book about zero-impact living
Colin Beavan

Living in an environmentally friendly way is easier said than done. What does it imply? What consequences does it have? How does it fit in with different aspects of our lives?

Colin Beavan (born 1963), a US non-fiction writer and internet blogger, and his family had the courage to try living a 'zero impact' lifestyle in New York City for one year. Read the following excerpt from Colin Beavan's report.

For one year, my wife, baby daughter, and I, while residing in the middle of New York City, attempted to live without making any net impact on the environment. Ultimately, this meant we did our best to create no trash (so no take-out food), cause
5   no carbon dioxide emissions (so no driving or flying), pour no toxins in the water (so no laundry detergent), buy no produce from distant lands (so no New Zealand fruit). Not to mention: no elevators, no subway, no products in packaging, no plastics, no air conditioning, no TV, no buying anything new … […]

10   My idea was to go as far as possible and try to maintain as close to no net environmental impact as I could. I aimed to go zero carbon – yes – but also zero waste in the ground, zero pollution in the air, zero resources sucked from the earth, zero toxins in the water. I didn't just want to have no carbon impact. I wanted to have no environmental
15   impact. […]

Stage one was trying to figure out how to live without making garbage: no disposable products, no packaging, and so on. Stage two involved traveling only in ways that emitted no carbon. In stage three, we would figure out how to cause the least environmental impact with
20   our food choices. Then we'd proceed through stages involving making as little environmental impact as possible in the areas of consumer purchases, household operations like heat and electricity, and water use and pollution. The whole thing would get harder and harder, or so I imagined, as we made each new adaptation.

25   I also decided I'd have to balance what negative impact we couldn't eliminate with some sort of positive impact. We would do this by cleaning up garbage in the Hudson River, helping care for newly planted trees, giving money to charity – environmental activism, maybe.

In blunt mathematical terms, in case you are an engineer or just
30   a geek who likes math, we would try to achieve an equilibrium that looked something like this

Negative Impact + Positive Impact = No Net Impact

This wasn't meant to be scientific so much as philosophical. Could we decrease our negative impact and increase our positive impact
35   enough so that they would balance out?

From: Colin Beavan, No Impact Man: Saving the Planet one Family at a Time, *2009*

Comprehension
1   **a**   Colin Beavan talks of the project in the form of a mathematical equation. Describe the formula in your own words.
    b   Give one example for each part of the equation (one positive and one negative).

3 net (adj) (here) indicating the damage to the environment when comparing the positive and negative factors **impact** ['ɪmpækt] results or effect of sth.
6 toxin ['tɒksɪn] poison **laundry detergent** [dɪ'tɜːdʒənt] soap made to wash clothes **produce** ['prɒdjuːs] (n) agricultural products such as fruits or vegetables
18 emit sth. [i'mɪt] (fml) diffuse or dischcarge sth. such as gas, light, etc.
30 geek (infml) nerd **equilibrium** [ˌiːkwɪ-'lɪbrɪəm, ˌekwɪ'lɪbrɪəm] state of equal balance (weight or forces)

Analysis

2 With a partner, compare and contrast the examples of negative and positive impact from the text. Which ones do you consider difficult or easy to achieve? Give reasons.

Beyond the text

3 Think about how your family treat the environment.

    a Evaluate what you could do as a family to reduce your negative impact and increase your positive impact.

    b Discuss what chances and challenges a low-impact lifestyle (or even a no-impact lifestyle) would entail for you.

4 `Mediating` Your English penfriend wants to take part in an international summer course on global environmental protection. In her application for a place on the course, she has to write an essay about waste reduction and prevention in Germany. She has found some information on the exhibition 'Zero Waste' at the *Museum der bildenden Künste* (Leipzig, 25.06.–08.11.2020). But it is too difficult for her and she has asked for help from someone who speaks German. Sum up the main points of the following text from the MdbK website for her.

MdbK   AUSSTELLUNGEN

Müll ist überall: als gigantischer Strudel im Pazifik, Feinstaub in der Luft und Mikroplastik in der Nahrungskette. Die Gruppenausstellung „Zero Waste" zeigt internationale Positionen zeitgenössischer Kunst, die auf die Dringlichkeit verweisen, Ressourcen zu schonen, weniger

5 zu konsumieren und nachhaltiger zu leben. In Installationen, Videos, Skulpturen und Fotografien untersuchen die beteiligten Künstler*innen globale Konsequenzen von Plastikverpackungen, Reifenabrieb, giftigen Chemikalien und Überproduktion. „Zero Waste" wird realisiert vom Umweltbundesamt in Kooperation mit dem MdbK und kuratiert

10 von Hannah Beck-Mannagetta und Lena Fließbach.

    Täglich verwehen Fetzen der als „mar de plástico" bekannten Gemüseplantagen in Südspanien ins Meer. Raul Walch dienen sie als Material für sein raumgreifendes Mobile. Das Künstlerduo Irwan Ahmett und Tita Salina überführt für seine Videoarbeit einen kleinen

15 Fisch von einem vermüllten Gewässer in Jakarta in einen kristall-klaren Fluss. Während Erik Sturm Feinstaub von Fensterbänken stark befahrener Straßen kratzt, um daraus Farbe herzustellen, führt

Swaantje Güntzel in ihren Fotografien und Objekten die Auswirkungen von Mikroplastik aus Kosmetikprodukten auf Meerestiere vor Augen. In seinem Labor experimentiert Dani Ploeger mit dem von Herstellern bewusst herbeigeführten Alterungsprozess elektronischer Geräte und Eliana Heredia arbeitet in ihrer Installation mit Wegwerfprodukten und Reinigungsmitteln.

Die Ausstellung möchte nicht nur einen kritischen Blick auf den aktuellen Zustand unserer Erde werfen, sondern Lösungsansätze diskutieren, zu alternativen Handlungsmöglichkeiten anregen und Visionen für die Zukunft entwerfen. Nicht zuletzt hinterfragt das Projekt auch den verschwenderischen Umgang mit Ressourcen in der Kunstwelt sowie den CO_2-Fußabdruck der Ausstellung selbst. […]

„Zero Waste" realisiert das Umweltbundesamt innerhalb seiner Programmreihe „Kunst und Umwelt". Wie können und wollen wir in Zukunft leben, ohne unsere Lebensgrundlage zu zerstören? Wie können wir lernen, neue Wege zu denken? Und wie kommen wir vom Wissen zum Handeln? Kunst und Kultur können einen wesentlichen Beitrag zum gesellschaftlichen Verständigungsprozess über Zukunftschancen und nachhaltige Entwicklung in unserer Gesellschaft leisten. Seit Mitte der achtziger Jahre pflegt das Umweltbundesamt, Deutschlands zentrale Umweltbehörde, deshalb mittels dieser Reihe den Dialog mit Kunstschaffenden.

From: the website of mdbk.de/ausstellungen

5 Compare the 'Zero Waste' exhibition and No-Impact Man (p. 68). How are their ambitions, chances and challenges similar and/or different?

A2 A mockumentary about plastic pollution

**Plastic bags are a relatively new item in grocery stores. They were not in common use until the 1980s.
But why have they become a major environmental concern?**

1 Think of a (nature) documentary film you have watched. With a partner, collect the typical features of nature documentaries and make a mind map. Consider the following questions:
   – Which topics are popular?
   – How are facts or stories communicated?
   – Are there protagonists? If so, how are they featured?
   – What about the setting?
   – What about sounds or noises?
   – Which other filmic elements are used?

Comprehension

2 **Viewing** Find the video 'The Majestic Plastic Bag' (2010) on the internet and watch it.
Give an outline of the events shown.

Analysis

3 Describe the cause-and-effect relation that is depicted in the video. Consider how the plastic bag is portrayed, its life cycle and the dangers and joys it experiences.

Make sure you understand these words and phrases from the video:
– plains (n)
– pupping ground (*Nährboden*)
– illustrious
– cycle of life
– migration
– release into the wild
– falter (v)
– be airborne
– garbage patch
– encounter sb./sth.
– talon (*Klaue, Kralle*)
– capture sth.
– pitch black
– phenomenal
– reed (*Schilfgras*)
– buoyancy (*Auftriebskraft*)
– thriving
– veritable
– current (n)
– biodegrade (v)
– coexist (v)
– species
– indigenous

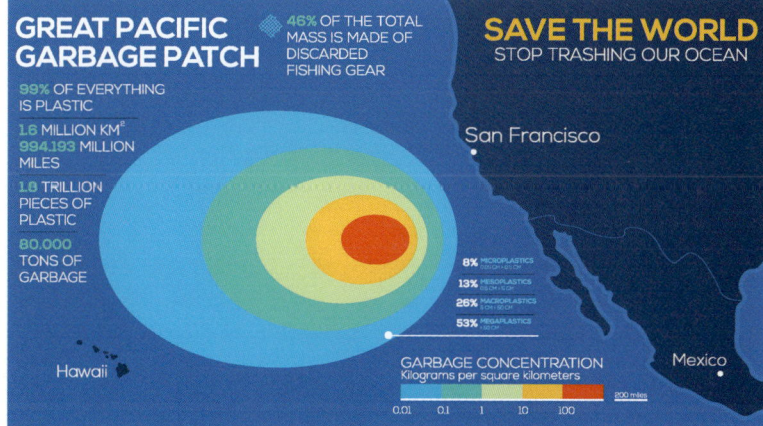

GREAT PACIFIC GARBAGE PATCH
46% OF THE TOTAL MASS IS MADE OF DISCARDED FISHING GEAR

SAVE THE WORLD
STOP TRASHING OUR OCEAN

99% OF EVERYTHING IS PLASTIC

1.6 MILLION KM²
994.193 MILLION MILES

1.8 TRILLION PIECES OF PLASTIC

80.000 TONS OF GARBAGE

San Francisco

8% MICROPLASTICS
13% MESOPLASTICS
26% MACROPLASTICS
53% MEGAPLASTICS

Hawaii

Mexico

GARBAGE CONCENTRATION
Kilograms per square kilometers
0.01 0.1 1 10 100   200 miles

The Great Pacific Garbage Patch: the largest accumulation of ocean plastic in the world

4 Many documentaries use storylines to arrange information. Use the table below to describe each feature of the storyline of 'The Majestic Plastic Bag'. Explain the function or effect the features have.

'The Majestic Plastic Bag'	Instances/Details	Function/Effect
Opening of the clip		
Voice/ Voice-over		
Creation of suspense		
Problem		
Resolution of the problem		

Info Mockumentary [ˌmɒkjuˈmentri]
The term 'mockumentary' brings together the verb 'mock' (= poke fun at, parody or satirize) and the noun 'documentary'. By blending the ideas contained in both words, it describes a film that makes invented events seem real. A mockumentary uses the features of a documentary, such as a serious tone and filmic features emphasizing the factuality of the given information about a chosen topic. At the same time, it uses satire or parody to both amuse viewers and wake them up to the fact that any kind of medium can be manipulated.

5

5 a Based on the Info box above, compare and contrast (nature) documentaries and mockumentaries.
b Explain how the video 'The Majestic Plastic Bag' qualifies as a mockumentary. Use the aspects and details you have analysed in **4** to support your argument.

Beyond the text
6 Look for other mockumentaries on the internet. Choose one and compare it to 'The Majestic Plastic Bag'.
7 Contemplate the problem of plastic waste throughout the world. What might be achieved by telling the story of the 'majestic bags' in a satirical way?

A3 Rap against climate change *Baba Brinkman*

Music is not necessarily a prime medium to communicate scientific facts, but it has the potential to trigger emotions. According to Canadian rapper Baba Brinkman, rap is the perfect language to get important messages across. He combines elements of rap and popular culture with scientific facts to raise people's awareness.

1 a `Viewing` Watch Baba Brinkman's song *I.P.C.C.* ($\rightarrow$ Info box below) without looking at the lyrics. Focus on his performance and on the interaction of words, images and music.

   b `Viewing` Watch the video again and highlight or underline all the words and phrases related to climate change.

Musician and rap artist Baba Brinkman (born 1978) performing at the Digital Life Design Conference in Munich in 2013

Info IPCC = Intergovernmental Panel on Climate Change (German 'Weltklimarat')
The IPCC is a United Nations body, founded in 1988, which assesses research on climate change, its natural, political and economic impacts as well as its risks. It suggests different solutions on how to adapt and respond to climate change. The IPCC does not carry out its own research, but rather publishes assessments, reports and methodologies based on
5 research from scientists around the world.

You want a new definition of 'hard core'?
Check out the intergovernmental climate
   report
It says the world is getting warmer,
5   unequivocally
And the oceans have increased 30 %
   in acidity
And 90 % of the warming trend is oceanic
And concentrated in the arctic – nobody
10   panic
But the level of greenhouse gasses in the air
Is higher now than it's been in millions of
   years
We added more than a trillion tonnes of
15   CO_2 to the atmosphere
It's gonna be centuries before some of the gasses clear
I'm dropping science, unvarnished, unbiased
But I don't blame you if your instinct is to deny it
'Cause we evolved to prioritize immediate threats
20 If it bleeds it leads, that's what the media says
So let the gangster-esque rap music paint a picture
And I'll hit you with some evidence-based predictions
Get ready for …

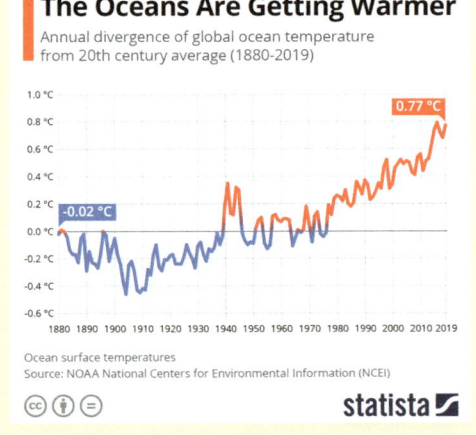

The Oceans Are Getting Warmer
Annual divergence of global ocean temperature
from 20th century average (1880-2019)

0.77 °C
-0.02 °C

Ocean surface temperatures
Source: NOAA National Centers for Environmental Information (NCEI)

statista

5 **unequivocally**
[ˌʌnɪˈkwɪvəkəli] (fml)
certainly, undoubtedly
7 **acidity** [əˈsɪdəti] (n) state
of containing acid *(Säure)*
17 **unvarnished** (fml)
(here) plain, honest
unbiased [ʌnˈbaɪəst]
not prejudiced or
influenced by opinions
18 **deny sth.** refuse to
accept sth. as true

Wars, famines, droughts, floods
25 **Hurricanes, heat waves, murders, thugs**
Chaos, refugees, stress, disease
Extinction, disaster, I-P-C-C

Hollywood summer blockbusters can't touch this
I get my thrills from the latest reports published
30 By the Intergovernmental Panel on Climate Change
Formed in 1988 to get the science straight
Now they dropped the fifth assessment and the data's up to date
So allow me to summarize: bad things on the way
Higher emissions, sea level rise, dire predictions
35 On target for disaster movie-style predicaments
In Copenhagen we set a limit of two degrees
But that's still enough to disintegrate major ice sheets
Over the course of centuries, or maybe decades
Yeah, some of the details are still up for debate
40 They fluctuate between certain disaster and likely disaster
Slow and steady or higher and faster
Consensus, it's the lowest common denominator
Which means it's probably gonna be way worse
Than the …

45 **Wars, […]**

So be afraid, be very afraid
But we're not, despite what the scenarios say
And the effect of talkin' about it is visible yawning
And occasionally changing our behaviour microscopically
50 And even those who get it, tend to get it logically
But not viscerally, so we're navigating myopically
The threat is existential, it's not environmental
And your individual response is inconsequential
Only coordination of our whole species
55 Is gonna keep coastal cities from sinking below the deep seas
And when was the last time a solution included all of us?
Geophysics is at the mercy of geopolitics
Climate change communicators, keep it positive
People need to feel like they still have options
60 And we do have options, either we find a solution
Or we stick with the business-as-usual level pollution
And get used to the …

Wars, […]

From: D. Brinkman and T. Caruana, The Rap Guide to Climate Chaos,
released 30 September 2016

---

[19] **evolve** [ɪˈvɒlv] develop over time
[22] **evidence-based** *beleg-bar, faktengestützt*
prediction [prɪˈdɪkʃn] *Prognose, Vorhersage*
[24] **drought** [draʊt] long period of time with little or no rain
[25] **thug** violent person, criminal
[32] **drop sth.** (here) publish sth.
assessment evaluation
[34] **dire** (fml) very serious
[35] **predicament** [prɪˈdɪkə-mənt] difficult or unpleasant situation
[36] **Copenhagen** location of the 2009 UN Climate Change Conference
[37] **disintegrate sth.** make sth. break up into very small pieces
[42] **common denominator** [dɪˈnɒmɪneɪtə] *gemein-same(r) Nenner*
[51] **viscerally** [ˈvɪsərəli] instinctively
myopically [maɪˈɒpɪkli] (fml) without seeing what the results of sth. will be
[53] **inconsequential** [ɪnˌkɒnsɪˈkwenʃl] unimportant
[57] **at the mercy of sb./sth.** not able to stop sb./sth. abusing you because they have power over you

Comprehension

2 Sum up the message of the song in a tweet (280 characters or less).

3 Create a mind map with the words and phrases you collected in **1b**. Use categories such as causes/consequences/dangers of climate change.

Analysis

4 Viewing Watch the video again. Focus on the features listed in the left-hand column of the table below. Write examples in the right-hand column.

Features of a scientific approach	IPCC report
Features of rap or pop culture	
Elements that raise climate change awareness	

Beyond the text

5 a Describe the chart on the right (→ Language help, p. 77).

b Analyse the message of the chart in relation to the message of Baba Brinkman's rap. Include the statistics from the graph on p. 74.

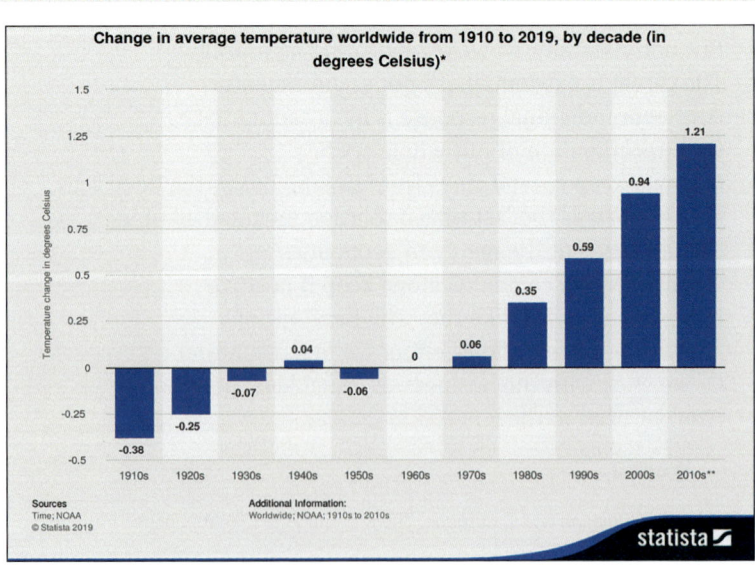

Change in average temperature worldwide from 1910 to 2019, by decade (in degrees Celsius)*

Temperature change in degrees Celsius

- 1910s: -0.38
- 1920s: -0.25
- 1930s: -0.07
- 1940s: 0.04
- 1950s: -0.06
- 1960s: 0
- 1970s: 0.06
- 1980s: 0.35
- 1990s: 0.59
- 2000s: 0.94
- 2010s**: 1.21

Sources
Time; NOAA
© Statista 2019

Additional Information:
Worldwide; NOAA; 1910s to 2010s

statista

Language help
The graph / bar chart … shows / deals with / is about … ·
The horizontal x-axis … and the vertical y-axis … · There are big/
vast/surprising differences between … · **up:** increase / rise /
go up · **down:** decrease / drop / fall / decline / go down ·
stable: remain constant/steady · **change** gradually/slightly/
gently/suddenly/sharply/steeply/dramatically · reach a peak /
the highest level · reach the lowest level

6 **Listening** Your teacher will play you an interview in which Baba
Brinkman talks about his songs and music. Listen and complete the
following sentences in your own words.

A Brinkman's target group is _____

_____

B According to Brinkman, saving water at home and taking the bike to work is _____

_____

C The lyrics of Brinkman's songs are 'peer-reviewed', which means that _____

_____

D For Brinkman, rap music is a powerful tool to get a message across, because _____

_____

7 **a** Some geographers and scientists believe that the environmental
impact of human activities on the Earth has become so severe that
we are living in a new geological epoch called the Anthropocene
(→ Info box below). Do some research and find arguments for
and against the idea of the Anthropocene.

b In groups of four, prepare a short debate in which two of you
present the arguments for the Anthropocene and the other two
present arguments against it.

c **Speaking** Hold your debate in front of the class.

Info Anthropocene [ˈænθrəpəsiːn, ænˈθrɒpəsiːn] (German 'Anthropozän')
The term 'Anthropocene' describes the current geological age, viewed as a period in which
humans started to have a new, irreversible impact on the climate and the environment.
Though widely used, the term is not officially accepted to describe geological time. Various
concepts propose different beginnings of the Anthropocene.

Part B
Music, art and nature

B1 Music and biology united *Björk*

The sounds of nature and music are closely related. They are often referred to as a universal language that is able to connect people and all living beings.

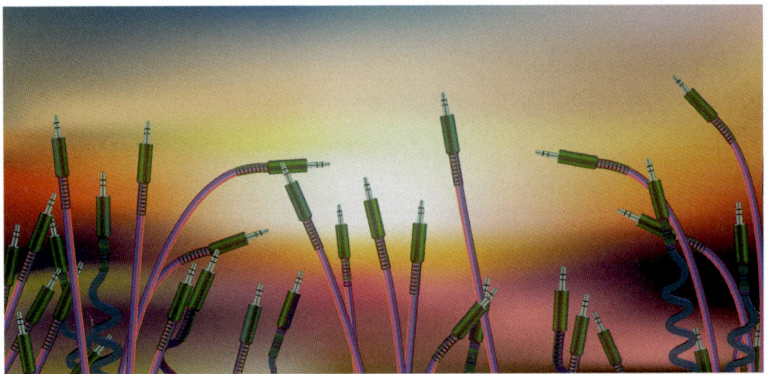

1 a Brainstorm elements in nature that make sound(s) or musical sound(s), e.g. thunder, fire.

Info Onomatopoeia [ˌɒnəˌmætəˈpiːə] (German 'Lautmalerei')
Onomatopoeia is the use of a word which imitates the sounds it refers to, e. g. *buzz* (bees) or *rumble* (thunder). In a group of words or a phrase it may evoke a particular feeling, mood, sound or movement.

---

b Explain what is meant by environmental noise. Give a few examples. State which noises annoy you most and why.

c Think of songs that you know in which sounds from nature are made electronically.

Your teacher will play a music video for you that links musical and biological processes.

Comprehension

2 Viewing Watch the video without sound.

   a Write down what you see (keywords) and what you associate with it.

   b Speculate: What could be the title of the song? What could be its theme? What style of music do you expect to hear?

   c Work with a partner. Compare and discuss your findings.

3 Viewing Watch the video with sound.

   a Pay special attention to the lyrics. Write down keywords that you hear.

   b Compare your findings to your ideas from **2b**.

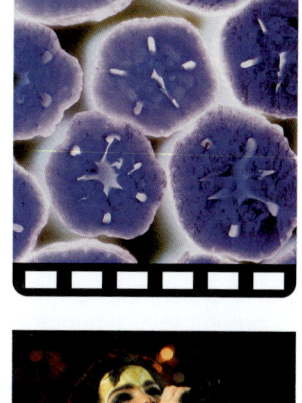

Analysis

4 Analyse how the themes of music, nature and technology are linked in the song. Explain how the artist uses musical sound (what kind?) and structure.

5 Read the lyrics that your teacher is going to give you. Analyse how the virus is represented through language and images.

Beyond the text

6 'Virus' is a song from the album 'Biophilia', which was released in 2011 by the Icelandic singer and songwriter Björk. With a partner, research and discuss the meaning of the word *biophilia*. Present your ideas.

Icelandic musician Björk (born 1965) performing in Rome in 2008

7 Compare the way the virus is depicted in the song/ video (which is from 2014) to representations of the COVID-19 coronavirus that was first reported in 2019 and became a pandemic.

8 **a** In groups of 4–5, create a sound montage (recording) of your favourite sounds from nature. You can either record sounds directly or use technical devices to produce a 'natural' sound.

   b Speaking Present your sound montage to the class. While listening to other groups' montages, take notes.

   c Discuss your works and give each other feedback.

B2 Environmental art

'We often forget that we are nature.
Nature is not something separate from us.
So, when we say that we have lost our
connection to nature, we've lost our
connection to ourselves.'

(Andy Goldsworthy, born 1956,
British sculptor and photographer)

1 In a gallery walk, your teacher is going to
present several quotations of artists to you.
With a partner, agree on a common message
of the quotations and write it down.

2 **a** With the help of different online sources, find
information about environmental art. Note down
typical characteristics.

b Imagine that you are putting together an exhibition about
environmental art. With a partner, brainstorm possible
artwork for the exhibition. Use your findings from **a** and
write down the defining features of your exhibits.

c **Speaking** Choose one piece of artwork that you would
like to include in your exhibition and present it to the
class. Explain why you chose it for your exhibition.

3 **a** You are going to work outdoors in groups. Your teacher
will give you the instructions and a list of items you have
to find.

b **Writing** In your group, write a short story (of no more
than 300 words) that connects all the objects from **a**.
Include vocabulary from nature.
Take turns in writing parts of the story.

c Read your story to the class.

Group 4
The Big Search

Please look for the
following things:
– a snail shell
– a blade of grass
– a piece of bark
– something totally
straight
– something which makes
a noise
– some litter

Protect the natural
environment.
Don't damage anything.

*Example instructions for the outdoor
activity 'The Big Search' (task 3a)*